CAMONICA VALLEY

A DEPICTION OF

VILLAGE LIFE IN THE ALPS

FROM NEOLITHIC TIMES TO

THE BIRTH OF CHRIST

AS REVEALED BY

THOUSANDS OF NEWLY FOUND

ROCK CARVINGS

1 9 6 1

ALFRED A. KNOPF   NEW YORK

CAMONICA VALLEY

EMMANUEL ANATI

TRANSLATED FROM THE FRENCH

BY LINDA ASHER

L. C. catalog card number: 61-14193

THIS IS A BORZOI BOOK,
PUBLISHED BY ALFRED A. KNOPF, INC.

FIRST AMERICAN EDITION

Originally published in French as
LA CIVILISATION DU VAL CAMONICA.
© B. Arthaud 1960.

TO MY TEACHERS

Professor R. Vaufrey

The Abbé H. Breuil

Foreword

NEITHER OUR WORK and our discoveries in the Camonica Valley nor the completion of this book would have been possible without the help of many teachers, colleagues, friends, and collaborators. To all of them I express my deep gratitude. I wish particularly to thank the Abbé Breuil and Professors Vaufrey, Vallois, Schaeffer, and A. Leroi-Gourhan for the interest they were kind enough to take in this research and for their spiritual and material help. In Italy, Professor M. Mirabella-Roberti, director of Antiquities of Lombardy; Professor A. C. Blanc, director of the Italian Institute of Paleontology; and the Cavaliere Bona, mayor of Capo di Ponte, all furnished valuable support during our investigations.

My deepest thanks go to my collaborators, French and Italian: R. Peroni, D. Brusardin, A. B. Rossi, G. Carbonnet, D. Pellard, and S. Christophe, who worked over the site with me; and to M. R. Pasquino, photographer at the Musée de l'Homme, who developed all the expedition's films. Also I wish to express deep thanks to Dr. Hugh Hencken, Director of the American School of Prehistoric Research, and to Christopher Hawkes, Professor of Prehistoric Archaeology at Oxford University, for having read and commented on the manuscript of the American edition of the present book.

Finally, I wish very specially to thank my friend Battista Mafessoli, who first showed me the Valley's graven rocks in the winter of 1956 and who accompanied me on my five subsequent expeditions.

For four consecutive years, through grants from the Excavations Commission of the Ministry of Foreign Affairs and from the National Center of Scientific Research, I was able to organize archaeological missions to the prehistoric sites of the Camonica Valley in the Italian Alps. Finally, in 1959, a grant of the American Philosophical Society enabled me to carry on a comparative study of north Italian and southeast French prehistoric art and to locate Val Camonica in this more general framework.

The results of these expeditions have previously been noted only in a few isolated articles, reports, and accounts in scientific journals. A description of carvings in the Paspardo region was published in 1957 in the *Bollettino di Paletnologia Italiana*; a short report on the first results, after our second expedition, was published in the American journal *Archaeology* (1957); and a first account of the economic foundations of Camunian society, written in 1957, was published in 1959 in the French journal *L'Anthropologie*. A report I gave before the Académie des Inscriptions et Belles-Lettres was published in 1959;[1] and *Scientific American* carried an illustrated account in early 1960.

[1] E. Anati: "L'art rupestre des Alpes Italiennes," *Académie des Inscriptions et Belles-Lettres* (1958), p. 192ff.

Meanwhile, we have begun to prepare for the complete publication of material collected during our expeditions; a comparative study and an analysis of the various documents will be included. This is, of course, a long project and will require several years of work. A first volume, written in 1957, appeared in January, 1961. It is entirely devoted to the study of a single rock of the six hundred in the Camonica Valley.[2]

This book is less ambitious; it does not claim to report—in the scientific sense—on the whole of our work. Rather, it is a response to a newly apparent desire for information on the part of a large audience and to the increasing interest the public has shown in archaeological research. Lengthy study is still necessary before definite conclusions can be reached, and the large-scale problems of continents and millennia are still far from resolved; but here, as elsewhere, perspectives open on vast masses of material until recently only suspected. It is these perspectives, these possibilities, or probabilities, that we have tried to outline here.

Forgotten for twenty centuries, Camunian civilization is only now coming back into history. There is a whole unknown people to rediscover, and we have only begun to pierce the night that still surrounds it.

E. A.

February 1961

---

[2] E. Anati: "La grande roche de Naquane," *Archives de l'Institut de Paléontologie humaine*, no. 31 (Paris; 1961), pp. 1-189, LII plates.

Contents

xi

CONTENTS

Illustrations
Maps
Charts

ILLUSTRATIONS, MAPS, CHARTS

xix

ILLUSTRATIONS, MAPS, CHARTS

CAMONICA VALLEY

1 · Introductory

WITHIN LESS than a century, the discovery of Paleolithic art at Altamira, at Trois-Frères, and then at Lascaux has given history a new dimension. Classical Greece and Rome, which had for generations marked the boundaries of our historical knowledge of Europe, became with this parade of refound millennia no more than a bright but brief instant in the duration and evolution of man.

But what significance has it for us, this flowering in southwest France and northern Spain that so far preceded the first civilizations of the ancient Mediterranean? How can we feel ourselves to be its heirs? Perhaps more than fifteen thousand years separate us from the Lascaux painters and from that underground sanctuary where unknown men came to enact their mysterious rites.

The Europe of the Ice Age was in a cultural stage that we

can define as savage. Seminomadic human bands hunted reindeer, bison and mammoth and lived in caves and rock shelters. Despite the marvelous works of art they have left behind, it is rather difficult to recognize in their way of life any of the foundations on which our own stands. We must allow that the ties which still bind us to them are very tenuous.

But when we consider the dawn of history in Europe, the great cultural assemblages which flourished in Mediterranean Europe, in Mycenae, and in Etruria, or in the Gallo-Celtic world, we realize that civilization, as we conceive it today, already possessed all its rules and attributes well before the birth of the Roman Empire. We realize that the key to our civilization is elsewhere, somewhere in the centuries between the end of the Ice Age and the beginnings of Greece and Rome. To know this period and to understand it would be to know and to understand ourselves.

What do we know to date, then, about the Europe of the last millennia before Christian times?

The discovery of the Mycenaean civilization stretched the limits of our information on Greece back a few hundred years; a constantly widening knowledge of the Etruscan has given us a clearer idea of the origins of Roman history. But these are Mediterranean peoples; study of them casts only an indirect light on continental prehistory. Of central and western Europe we know very little.

Until the generation of our fathers, our chief source of information on the customs of the pre-Roman peoples of the continent had been the Latin or Greek authors, whose descriptions, though often brightened with picturesque touches, are not always reliable. Not only are their references fragmentary; they suffer besides from a kind of distortion because their subjects are considered exotic—bizarreness is expected

4

of them and it has virtually no limits but those of the imagination.

During the past sixty years, however, our knowledge has been broadened by a number of archaeological discoveries. Excavations have familiarized us with the different types of pottery used in Neolithic Europe, then in the Bronze and Iron Ages. We have also learned the various techniques of the different peoples who inhabited the continent—for example, their methods of metalworking. In certain cases, some of the religious ideas of these peoples—their conception of death, among others—are revealed to us by their necropolises. But about their dwelling places we have so far no more than vague, often hypothetical, notions. Only in the realm of technology and the contacts that these prehistoric populations established among themselves or with regions outside Europe, do we have much information, as witness the multitude of scientific articles and books dedicated to the subject. Such eminent authorities as V. Gordon Childe and Grahame Clark have been able to arrange the available data so as to cast satisfactory light on the area of material culture.

But how much do we know about the daily life, the mythology, the ritual, and the religious beliefs of those times? What do we know of the social and economic organization of the tribes who occupied Europe between the Stone Age, for example, and the advent of the great pre-Roman cultural units of the Celtic type?

The uncovering of a unique collection of works of art in a lost furrow of the Italian Alps, in the Camonica Valley, contributes a mass of new data to the problem. For this time we are not dealing with isolated finds, with a pile of debris or shards, with an array of weapons in a tomb, or with simple building foundations. Here we have a large quantity of com-

5

plex representations showing persons in their own environment, engaged in the ordinary activities of daily life. Each carving is a document on the economic system, the social organization, and the beliefs of the people who engraved them.

Even detached from its context, and so to speak isolated in space, this discovery would hold great interest; the testimony it presents on a human community of the second and first millennia before our era is in itself of considerable significance. What makes the find exceptionally important, however, is that, situated as it is, it bears on other regions of Europe where excavations have so far provided us with only an incomplete image of the same period. The Valley seems to be a kind of archaeological reserve where we can see a culture in its totality and diversity. Elsewhere in prehistoric Europe, culture is revealed to us only in sparse fragments, often difficult to relate to each other and even harder to reconstruct as a whole. Great problems of protohistory, like that of the origin of the Celts, for example, derive new light through this discovery. Just as in many cases it would have been difficult, if not impossible, to decipher the carvings in the Valley without reference to findings made elsewhere, a mass of questions hitherto ill resolved have found answers in the Camonica Valley. One need only mention the instance of the pile dwellings: a great many remains have been found in the Alpine regions, but the vestiges are limited to the wooden or stone foundations that supported them. Under the best conditions, it has been possible to deduct an approximate plan for these primitive houses but never to determine their general appearance. We were forced to make hypothetical attempts at reconstructions; the architecture remained a mystery. The Valley engravings, showing houses and huts, and showing them full front, elevated, with roofs, roof coverings, entrances, and stairs, are obviously irreplaceable documents toward the solution of this mystery.

One could list many similar examples. Such analogies are valid not only in the field of material culture but in other areas as well—religious, social, economic, and so on. The discoveries in the Camonica Valley have a significance far beyond their local framework. Thanks to them, the line is established between Stone Age Europe and Roman times, between prehistory and history. And in the Camonica Valley this line flows without interruption, summing up in a single site all the subsequent steps taken by man: from a savage cultural level dependent mainly on hunting and gathering, through gradually evolving stages of barbarism based on a more complex economy and on richer and more varied ideology, to urban civilization, literacy, and historic thought and philosophy.

In this connection, what do we mean by history and prehistory? What distinguishes the two terms? Some authors define history as that period of human evolution which begins with writing. But we know that writing began at widely different times in various parts of the world. It was already in use in some countries of the East and the Mideast three thousand years before Christ; yet it appeared in northern Europe only around the start of our era.

Moreover, is it not true that civilizations possessing writing have relapsed into dark ages from which no written contemporary document has come down to us? Even in Europe, have not the great barbaric invasions occasionally meant, in certain regions, a veritable return to prehistory?

If we abandon this chronologic criterion and rely on sources and means of knowledge, we find that the dividing line is not much clearer. What we know of some epochs which are fairly familiar because they belong, in the strongest sense of the term, to history, varies strangely and may swing from the very certain to the very doubtful, when indeed we are not forced to confess total ignorance. Written history, as Gordon Childe says, is no more than the very fragmentary and incomplete account of what men have done in some areas of the world during the last five thousand years. More often than not, annals, archives, official documents of all kinds are valuable guides for learning the succession of kings or the number of victories won by a famous warrior, but they tell us very little about the country where these events occurred, about its inhabitants, the life they led, their economic and social organization, their beliefs, superstitions, or thought. Or, conversely, an archaeological discovery may reveal a host of details on these subjects, permitting us to reconstruct rather accurately the way of life of a certain society, yet leaving us in the dark about the other aspects. If writing was unknown, we can learn neither the names of the kings nor those of the gods whom the rediscovered people worshipped.

This is the case in the Camonica Valley. The only inscriptions found there date from the last period of Camunian art; that is, from the time Rome flourished. But at that time exterior political, economic, and cultural influences had already begun to make themselves strongly felt, and soon thereafter the antique civilization of the Valley foundered and disappeared. For two thousand years before, the Camunians lived a calm and industrious life in their lost Alpine valley, successfully preserving their economic and cultural autonomy. All that we know of those two thousand years is recounted to us by twenty thousand carvings on rocks. But these invaluable documents, despite all the uncertainties that still surround them, reveal much more about the civilization of the Camonica Valley than we know about its inhabitants from the time of the Roman conquest to the end of the Middle Ages. Can we, then, speak of that civilization in terms of history or prehistory? Let us say we are dealing with the history of a prehistoric society.

The important fact is that already discernible in that new world at birth is an image much like our own. The existence of the Camunians, it will be seen, had a great deal in common with that of the medieval peasants; nor was it very different from the life certain rural populations of Europe lead today. In addition, the origins of certain popular beliefs and legends that have sometimes persisted into our own times are revealed by the Camunian pictures. Through them we also recognize rites and beliefs which were adopted and transformed by the Etruscans and by Rome and whose true age had gone unsuspected. As remarkable as are the numerous other rock-picture sites of Europe, including those in Mount Bego in the French Maritime Alps, those in Scandinavia or in eastern Spain, none of them bears comparison with the Camonica Valley, either for the variety of subjects represented or for the ethnologic interest of the documentation. In the Valley the graven rocks tell more than just the history of a people living a rustic life; through this people they offer us two thousand years of an all but unknown world.

2 · The Site

LOCATION OF THE VALLEY AND THE
ARCHAEOLOGICAL REMAINS

THE CAMONICA VALLEY, a wide, deep fault almost 50 miles long, open at the heart of the Italian Alps in a magnificent setting of high mountains and glaciers, lies north of the city of Brescia, between Lake Iseo and the Swiss frontier. Its altitude ranges from some 650 feet above sea level at the lake to about 5,500 feet at the Tonale Pass, at the northernmost end. The Oglio river carves its bed through the Valley, grows fatter from numerous tributaries, and empties into Lake Iseo. Now developed all along its course, the Oglio has completely transformed the appearance and the economy of the region. Where today one finds an electric power station, factories, mills, well-cultivated fields, and a whole irrigation system, once there spread a vast marshland, with small stagnant lakes where the Valley widened and its slopes grew gentler. Two thousand years ago Roman engineers must have given up the idea of building a road on the Valley floor; the one they finally made clings to the mountain sides and overlooks the river from a height of 250 feet. Today's inhabitants live along that road and have built modern villages on the same sites as the ancient ones.

The prehistoric villages were not at the bottom of the Valley either, but scattered above it here and there. Some few vestiges of human habitation have also been found on the surrounding hills: dry walls of large stones, pottery fragments, stone mortars, millstones, and pestles.

Map showing distribution of rock carvings and menhir statues in northern Italy.

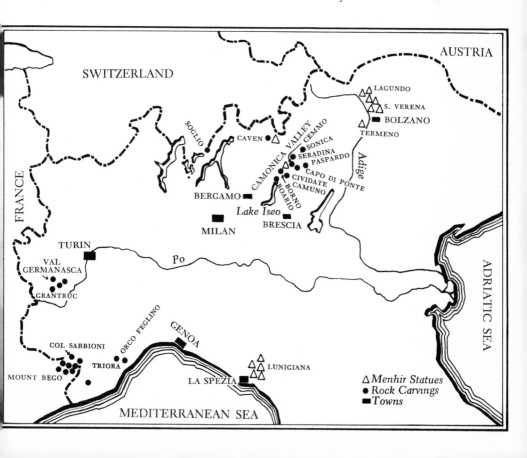

But the Camonica Valley appears relatively poor in archaeological remains other than the rock carvings. A small necropolis belonging to the second Iron Age and dating from the fifth and sixth centuries B.C. was excavated near the village of Breno by three Italian prehistorians, Bertolone, Bonafini, and Rittatore.[1] Recently, in the region called *delle Sante*, near an important group of rock carvings, what seems to be the basement of a rampart wall and some ceramic shards were unearthed by another archaeologist, Dr. Renato Peroni; these probably date from the late Bronze Age. A few years ago in a sounding the excavation division of the Brescia Museum found some Bronze Age pottery; in 1933 Professor Giovanni Marro discovered near Breno[2] a Bronze Age ax; and other bronze tools were recovered at other spots in the Valley and are now collected in a small museum in the town.[3]

Besides these antiquities, we also find dry walls scattered in the woods and ravines around the Camonica Valley. Some of these walls, like those studied on two hills in the *delle Sante* region, seem to come from *castellieri*, or small fortified villages built around the fourth and third centuries B.C. and belonging to the late Iron Age. There are also a few structures cut into the rocks (stairs, cup marks, tiny canals probably designed to catch or distribute rain water, and the like). This is the meager extent of our documentation. Without the rock carvings we would know very little, almost nothing, of the life and history of the Valley's inhabitants before the Roman conquest.

[1] Bertolone, Bonafini, Rittatore: "La necropoli preromana di Breno in Val Camonica," *Sibrium*, Vol. III (Varese, 1953), pp. 73-8.

[2] G. Marro: "Un'ascia di bronzo della Valcamonica," *Atti della Reale Accademia delle Scienze di Torino*, Vol. LXIX (1933-4).

[3] Bonafini: *Il Museo di Breno in Valcamonica* (Breno; 1955).

View of the Camonica Valley.

DISCOVERY OF THE ROCK ART IN
THE CAMONICA VALLEY

The old civilization of the Camonica Valley having disappeared utterly with the arrival of the Romans, the subsequent generations forgot the meaning and even the existence of the prehistoric engravings. Yet they remained, scarcely dulled by time. To the eyes of later populations unable to guess their origin, they must soon have come to be considered the work of sorcerers, fairies, and evil spirits, the mysterious signs of

13

dangerous forces requiring immediate exorcism. Such assumptions were quite probably the basis for the much more recent crosses we find on the rocks near the carvings.

Eventually, though, the markings were forgotten; moss and earth crept over them. But the old fears persisted along with the phantasms they had engendered. Through the centuries a shadow of their memory survived in the traditions, the folk tales, and even the place names of the region. Thus, a hill near the village of Sonico, where some carvings were found, is called the Fairy Horn, the *Corno delle Fate*; and a rise overlooking the valley is the *Cima delle Streghe*, the Witches' Peak.

One rock remained partly uncovered, however, and the people of the village of Cemmo knew of it. In 1914 some

First rock discovered in the Camonica Valley at Cemmo, subject of a report by Professor Laëng in 1914. Compare with illustration on p. 59.

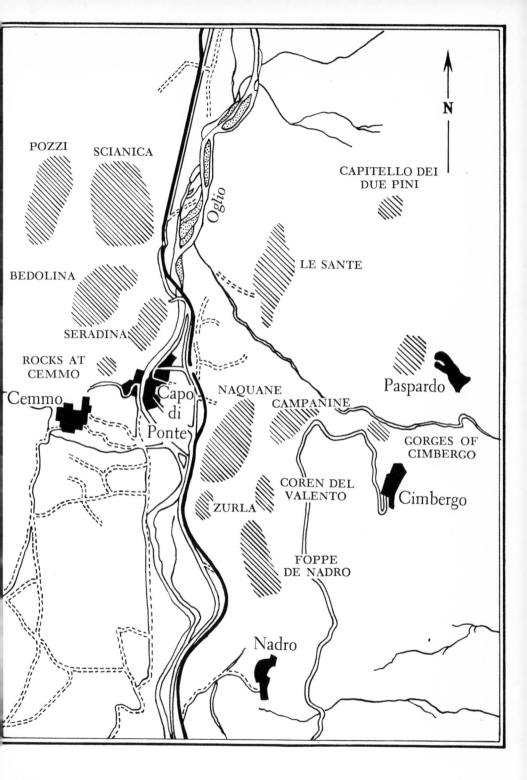

POZZI

SCIANICA

CAPITELLO DEI
DUE PINI

Oglio

BEDOLINA

LE SANTE

SERADINA

ROCKS AT
CEMMO

Paspardo

Cemmo

Capo
di
Ponte

NAQUANE

CAMPANINE

GORGES OF
CIMBERGO

COREN DEL
VALENTO

Cimbergo

ZURLA

FOPPE
DE NADRO

Nadro

N

Sites of rock carvings near the village of
Capo di Ponte in the Camonica Valley.

shepherds showed it to Professor Guattiero Laëng, of Brescia, who later reported it to the Italian Speleological Society. Then for fifteen years no more attention was paid to it. In 1930 interest revived, and the rock was entirely uncovered by two Italian scholars, Professors Paolo Graziosi and Giovanni Marro, who then undertook its study.[4] In the same year Marro discovered another engraved rock. Two years later, still others were found near Capo di Ponte, a village near the Naquane area, this time by Giovanni Marro and Raffaello Battaglia.

There followed during 1932-36 a long discussion between these two archaeologists, each attempting, in a series of articles published in scientific journals, to win acceptance for his theory. They were not then concerned with interpreting or understanding the carvings, and in most cases publication simply meant description. The discussion had to do primarily with the dating of the carvings.

The discovery in 1954 of still another carved rock near the village of Borno called archaeologists' attention once again to the Camonica Valley and awakened the curiosity of the scholarly world. Immediately prospectors set to searching the valley right and left, and the discoveries multiplied. Guattiero Laëng, Emanuele Süss, Sabina Fumagalli, and others found some twenty engraved rocks. These findings were publicized in the newspapers and increased scientific interest in the Valley still more.

Meanwhile, a carpenter from Capo di Ponte, Battista Mafessoli, fascinated by these investigations, began to spend all his free time in the woods searching for new carvings. He

---

[4] P. Graziosi: "Le incisioni preistoriche di Val Camonica," *Archivio per l'antropologia et l'etnologia,* Vol. LIX (Florence, 1931), pp. 105-112. G. Marro: "Arte rupestre zoomorfica in Valcamonica," *Rivista di Antropologia,* Vol. XXIX (Rome, 1930).

soon became something of an expert, and his practiced eye recognized countless figures previously unnoticed on rocks that had already been examined.

It was then, in the winter of 1956, that I came to the Camonica Valley for the first time. I wished to compare the carvings I had seen in the different journals with those I was studying at that time on Mount Bego in the French Maritime Alps. I was put in touch with Battista Mafessoli; together we roamed endlessly through the woods and ravines of the place, and I saw the carvings. Of most of the rocks, only small patches showed above the earth; the bulk of the rocks disappeared beneath the grass and moss. It seemed probable that the engravings continued underground, and this proved to be so when I scraped away the soil and grass around one of the rocks. The newly cleaned section showed other carvings. Continuing our search, we soon discovered, around the zones already prospected, more rocks unknown till then and entirely covered with all kinds of figures. Under the moss and growth of the slopes there existed an enormous prehistoric collection, an inestimable artistic treasure.

I had intended to spend no more than a day in the Camonica Valley. I stayed a week. At the end of that time the number of rocks found in the valley had doubled. I had taken a few photographs and made some tracings, but that was only a beginning; more profound study was required.

I went to see Professor Battaglia, a prominent scholar interested in the Valley's engravings, and I told him what I had found. He encouraged me to go on with my research, and together we tried to figure out where in the Valley the most important concentrations of rock pictures were located. I realized that Battaglia was at the time one of the few scholars aware of the archaeological and ethnological importance of the Valley. However, he kindly advised me to consult a high

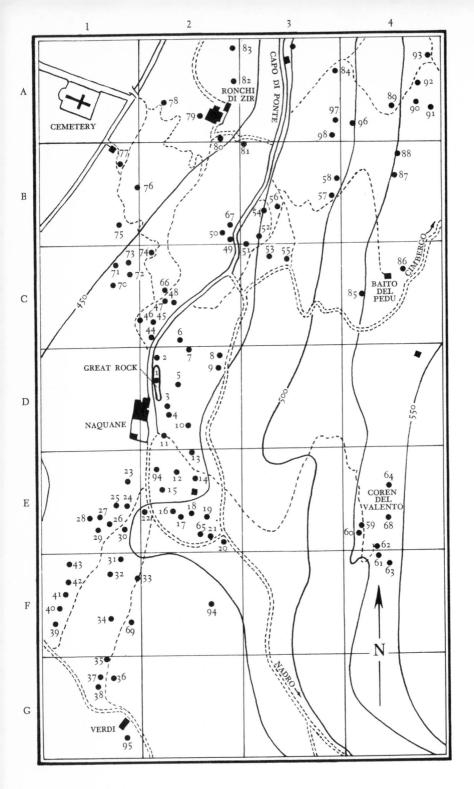

May showing the distribution of carved
rocks in the Naquane region of the Camonica Valley. By E. Süss.

school teacher in Brescia, Emanuele Süss, who had been surveying various areas of the Valley. A friendly and collaborative relationship developed between us, and I found in Süss one of the most passionate searchers for rock pictures.

Directly upon my return to Paris, I showed my tracings and snapshots to the Abbé Breuil, to Professor Vaufrey, Professor Schaeffer, and other eminent archaeologists; all of them evidenced a great interest and urged me to return to Italy to study the Valley carvings.

My first expedition to the Camonica Valley was accomplished entirely with volunteers, painters and friends from Montparnasse who were excited about the investigation and agreed to spend their vacations with me, looking for prehistoric Italian art. Under these conditions, of course, it was impossible to begin excavations: all we could do was clean the rocks above the surface and trace and photograph their carvings.

Methodical work, clearly, was difficult; classification, photographs, tracings, and sketches required a team of specialists—which was sorely lacking. Nonetheless, we brought back to Paris enough tracings and photos for a report with which to arouse interest. That first campaign gave us, moreover, some idea of the immense number of prehistoric carvings to be found in the Camonica Valley and of their whereabouts, as well as of the significance of the discovery from the viewpoint of archaeology and ethnology.

The material collected in the course of that first expedition finally won us a few small grants. They were enough to buy the tools we needed for our next mission. The Camonica expedition was going ahead; the work proceeded and acquired a normal rhythm. In 1958 we had the assistance of various Italian institutions as well. Thanks to the Lombardy Direction of Antiquities and its director, Professor Mirabella-Roberti, and also to the kindness of the Cavaliere Bona, mayor of Capo di Ponte, workers were made available to help us uncover new rocks and excavate around them. Professor A. C. Blanc, director of the Istituto di Paletnologia Italiana, sent us the welcome and stimulating help of Dr. Peroni. Finally, the work of summarizing, of comparing and relating Val Camonica to other areas and art groups, was part of a research project to whose support the American Philosophical Society contributed.

Today nearly six hundred engraved rocks are known to us, including over twenty thousand rock pictures spread over an area fifty miles long. Most of this material has been fully traced, copied, photographed, and analyzed.

3 · Work Methods

IT IS OFTEN SAID that it is results that count. I am not entirely sure of the general truth of the maxim, but I do not believe it applies to archaeology. For the methods employed have an enormous influence on the results, and only when we know how the work was done can we evaluate the end product. This is why I feel it necessary to devote a whole chapter to our research methods in the Camonica Valley. The reader will then have a better idea of the raw material we are dealing with and of the processes by which finally we were able to analyze and correlate the documentary evidence collected. Because of the new problems presented, the rock pictures of the Camonica Valley demanded new techniques quite different from those ordinarily used in archaeology.

Every student of archaeology knows how to plot a terrain and excavate a site; he also knows how to go about analyzing fragments of pottery or flint tools; nor is he at a loss when it comes to integrating such finds into a logical framework so that certain conclusions may be drawn from them. But the study of rock art is infinitely more complex, for here we have to deal not with objects themselves but with pictures of objects and sometimes with the representation of totally intangible realities. Rock art is also a more recent area of study; people are only beginning to be actively interested, so that there are few specialists with experience in the particular techniques called for. The world has been interested for more than a hundred and fifty years in the paintings and carvings discovered in the Egyptian pyramids and in the Etruscan tombs; their monumental nature and their occurrence in remarkable architecture could not fail to grip the attention of scholars. But the often minuscule carvings or scarcely visible paintings on scattered rocks in obscure valleys have too frequently been considered, even by experts, with mistrust and scepticism. They were impossible to date, it was said; or they were only the scribblings of children; or they were made casually by random shepherds with no particular purpose in mind. The rare scholars who were interested, even when suspecting the importance of that mass of iconographic documents, were dis-

Cleaning and brushing before tracing.

couraged by the schematic, monotonous character of the figures. This is not true of the Camonica Valley, where the scenes are engraved in realistic style and with great precision of detail.

The procedure we started with was that used in any excavation: the carvings had to be analyzed from technical, artistic, and stylistic standpoints, just as ceramic shards or flint tools are. But then a means had to be found to relate each subject to its particular scene; to make comparative studies of the different scenes and the various techniques and styles; and eventually to understand correctly the whole meaning of this prehistoric method of expression. The reader will see in the following pages how we succeeded. Our procedure is the culmination of a long development by which research experience on art sites in the Middle East, in Spain, and elsewhere was adapted to the special case of the Camonica Valley art.

FIELD WORK

Not all the carved rocks in the Valley were underground, but moss carpeted them thickly and hid the strange designs from view. In the case of such stones, a stiff brushing was sometimes enough to reveal the carvings. As for the others, entirely submerged under earth torn from the mountains by centuries of erosion, chance alone brought them to light. One, for instance, was dredged up during the construction of a road; it had been about six feet underground.

Rocks dug up from below the surface are of course the

23

Working on the rock.

easiest to clean; simply flushing them with water is enough
to bring out the designs. Rocks that have remained above
ground in their original position are generally badly weathered
and their incisions are less sharp. Moreover, they are frequently coated with a fine moss, rock mushrooms, lichens,
and other microscopic plants which are extremely hard, if not
impossible, to scrape off entirely. When stiff scouring brushes
and prolonged, repeated washings did not avail, we used very
fine blades and dental instruments—and immense patience.

Some of the carvings are deep and very clear, while others

are scarcely visible; to bring them out more sharply and be able to study the whole more easily we had to employ either of two different techniques. One is well known: it consists of projecting light across the rock at such an angle that all the irregularities, and of course the incisions, are thrown into relief. But this process is only feasible on smooth flat rocks, and it presents certain difficulties, not the least of which is transporting an electric generator and projectors into the mountains.

It is apparent, then, why we preferred the other method. In this, the rock is covered with a coat of very dilute *gouache*. Then, when the rock is dry, it is wiped over with a damp cloth; the paint vanishes from the smooth surface leaving a faint tint only in the incisions. The carvings stand out clearly and can easily he examined, traced, and photographed. This process has the added advantage that it brings out a wealth of small details that would otherwise escape detection. This was, therefore, the method we used most often. But to obtain satisfactory results it was often necessary to repeat the same operation many times. Once it took a four-man team four days to clean and prepare a rock some fifty yards long.

After this initial work was finished and the rocks prepared, their surface was sectioned off by a grid into rectangles the size of our tracing sheets (about 30 x 39 inches). The rock was first divided into two parts along a north-south axis. The perpendicular lines were numbered from south to north. The parallels going west from the axis were designated by letters, beginning with A; the parallels east of it were also lettered, but beginning with Z. This plan would allow the expansion of the grid in all the necessary directions if new carvings were discovered beyond our starting area.

Grid plan of the great Naquane rock, showing carved areas.

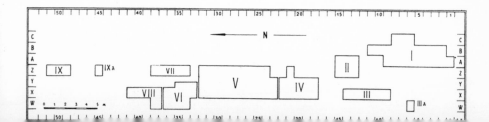

Many of the engravings on the Valley's rocks are super-imposed on one another. The sequence of the layers is clearly of great interest to the student of the evolution of Camunian art. To trace them, we used inks of different colors. In this way, when the work was done and the tracings tacked up on the laboratory walls, it was a simple matter to find our way among them.

In the laboratory the tracings were reduced on a scale of $\frac{1}{10}$ for the larger rocks and $\frac{1}{5}$ for the smaller. Even so, some of our diminished reproductions are more than five yards long.

Final operation: photography. For each rock we took an over-all photograph; then a mosaic of shots in vertical sequence; and, lastly, details. The photos for our horizontal mosaic were all taken at the same distance, with the lens held perpendicular to the center of the squares so that each square has a margin of four to five inches on all sides. By means of this margin we were able later to piece together a total image of each rock.

Both photographs and tracings are obviously necessary since they are used differently. How many times were we obliged to trace off superimposed carvings, using a magnifying glass to untangle the lines! In those cases our photos were useless. Moreover, the differences between the angles of focus at the center and at the edges of the photograph create a certain amount of discrepancy when the different parts of the total are interrelated. Nevertheless, the photographs constitute an indispensable complement of information as well as an additional safeguard. In reducing the tracings, for example, the draftsman may hesitate over a poorly defined or unfinished line. He then has recourse to the photos. The over-all photographic composites bring out the small details that might not always be clearly noticeable in the tracings.

Tracing the designs outlined in chalk.

They are essential in studying the way the carvings were executed, in examining the minutiae of a line or a figure, in distinguishing among different kinds of chiseling or pecking, or in comparing the particularities of two patinas.

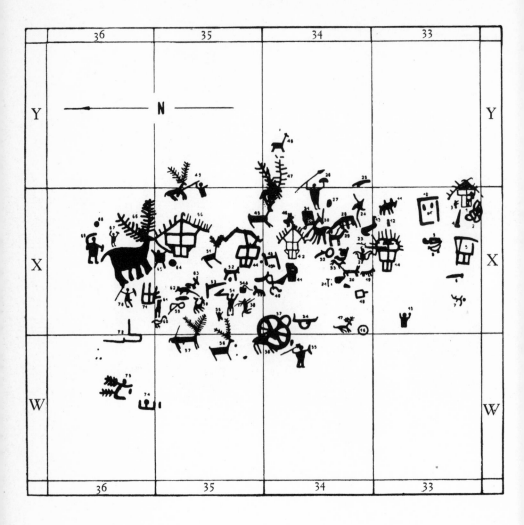

Area VI of the great Naquane rock. The carvings in this area are executed in different styles and by various techniques, but analysis and grouping bring out scenes and compositions.

28

Scene from area VI of the great Naquane rock, showing stag worship. A single technique was used in these carvings, which form a composition. Compare with the whole array of carvings in the same area as shown in the preceding illustration.

29

We also had a moving picture camera with us. The director, Sam Itzkovitch, and the cameraman, Denis Clerval, were thus able to film the high points of our investigations and to record the different phases of our work, from the discovery of a new rock through the examination, analysis, and interpretation of its carvings.

Evenings, when the day's work at the site was done, the laboratory work would begin. The carvings had been photographed and traced; now they were numbered, described in detail, and classified. The classification of our copies was made first by the rock they came from and then by the subject of the carving. This allowed us to establish, as we went along, a comparison between the new material and carvings from previous investigations and to begin without further delay on the analysis and the synthesis of our findings.

ANALYZING THE CARVINGS

The carvings of the Camonica Valley, which represent human figures with their tools and weapons and their domestic animals, in their houses and in all kinds of other scenes, provide the most vivid and positive testimony on the activities and the way of life of the region's ancient populations. Each carving is a little tableau, naïve but precise, full of picturesque details; together they display to us an existence that disappeared more than two thousand years ago.

But the Camunian civilization hid its secret well. If we have been able to learn something about it, it is at the price of many hard months of analysis, research, correlation, and comparison. Only by examining the patinas over the carvings, the chiseling techniques used by the prehistoric artists,

30

the different subjects that inspired them, the geographic distribution of the graven rocks—only after such meticulous scrutiny have we come to know something about the people who left us the carvings.

Next we had to reduce our tracings to a smaller scale. Not till this was accomplished did the constructive part of our work begin. The detailed and segmented study of our material allowed us to establish statistics, to determine rules that would relate the carvings to each other, and thence to try to understand their meaning and their purpose. Then we might try to interpret the evidence they present on the life and thought of the men who made them.

The rock art of the Camonica Valley is not static like much of its kind—that at Mount Bego, for example, or in the Negev. The engraver, even in the most schematic phases of this art, always gives evidence of his personality. Each figure and subject, even if it resembles others, is different from them in some respect. The classification of our copies would have presented an almost insuperable problem if we had wished to take these differences into account always and everywhere. We preferred, rather, to simplify the task by classing the material from the start—which at the same time would facilitate its analysis. We decided, therefore, to gather the collected figurations under twelve chapter headings, or general groups, in the following order:

1. *Human figures*
2. *Animals*
3. *Buildings and huts*
4. *Vehicles*
5. *Plows*
6. *Looms*
7. *Weapons and tools*

31

8. *Nets and traps*
9. *Labyrinths*
10. *Feet and hands*
11. *Geometric designs and abstract figures*
12. *Inscriptions and alphabetic characters*

In passing, let me note that we succeeded in isolating twenty-eight different types of human figures, for instance, and nine major kinds of animals, fourteen kinds of geometric signs, and so on.

By grouping under the same heading figure types with

Scenes of war. Warriors armed with lances and shields, style IV, overlaid with paddles and other motifs. The animals in linear style are the more ancient.

rather similar meanings, or those of which we found only a few examples, we were able to limit the basic categories to seventy; this in turn made it possible to organize our subdivisions on perforated sheets. These sheets permit the instant selection of all the figures pertaining to any one subject; without them minute and complete study of the thousands of figures we had collected would have been impossible. They work in this way: the card is perforated all along the border, and each hole represents a different subject. On each card is the detail photograph of a group of engravings, with the hole or holes corresponding to that group notched on the outside. To pick out all the carvings representing a certain subject, one has only to insert a small rod into the corresponding perforation and pull out the sheets. Whatever comes out of the bundle is the pertinent documentation.

More complex and detailed systems of analysis and synthesis cards are possible, of course, but this simple method does not require IBM machines and can be used anywhere by anyone. For us it was important to resolve the problem of simplification. We wanted every member of the expedition to participate actively in the processes of detection, collection, analysis, synthesis, and interpretation. But we had with us students, amateurs, and people who had never before dealt with archaeology or anthropology. Whatever was to be done had to be clearly understandable to all.

We do not regret the simplification. In fact, our method is today understood by everyone and applied by every archaeologist, student, or amateur who has seen us working in the field. Our cards and files have nothing arcane about them, and the possibility of a mistake is rare. Italian peasants and other country people have consulted them, contributed to their content, and done some of the work they called for.

The file sheets, classified according to the rock, the loca-

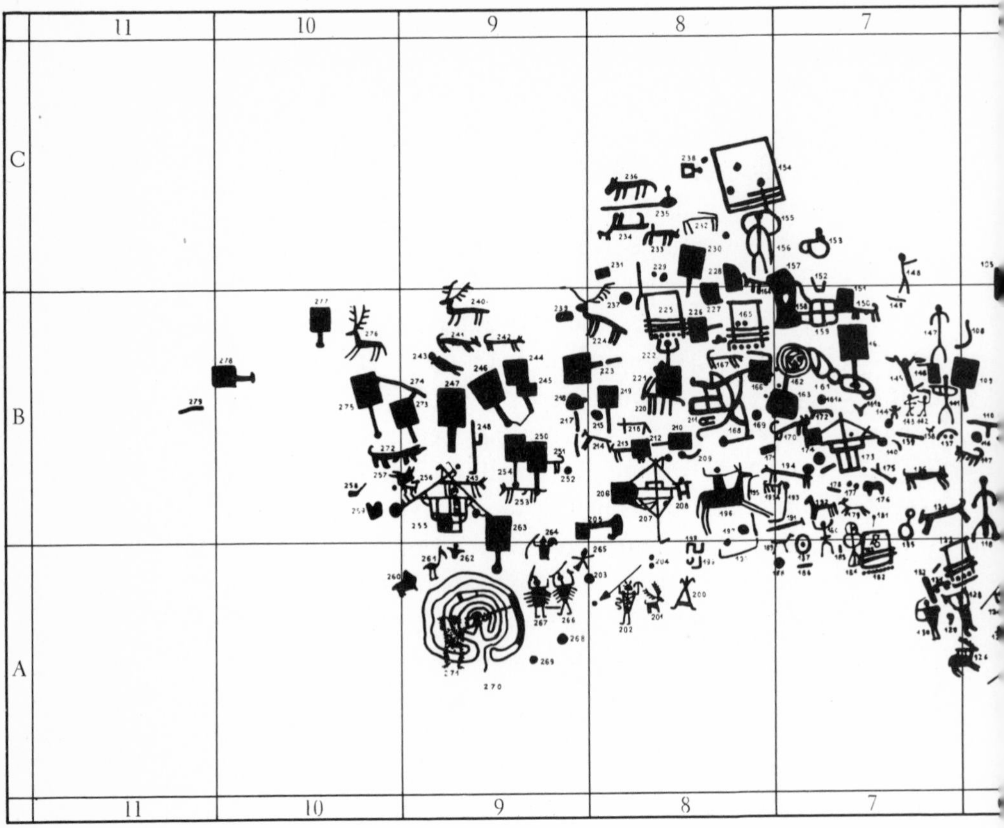
11
10
9
8
7
C
B
A

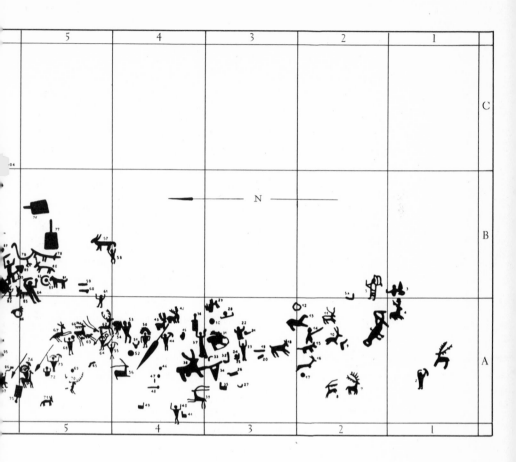

Area I of the great Naquane rock. Many of the scenes are superimposed on earlier carvings (see p. 43).

tion, and the area they came from, give an immediate breakdown and distribution of the various subjects in the different sites. This system of classification enables the researcher to discern in each rock the particular characteristic that distinguishes it from the others, to detect the clear predominance of one subject or, in many instances, of a certain type of scene which may be repeated in succession and prevail over the rest. In the large rocks, the same subject may be found on different parts of the graven surface. Look, for example, at the table of subject distribution for the great rock of Naquane, on page 37. This rock, which is fifty-two yards long, bears eight hundred eighty-five carvings, divided into nine sectors. The repertory of figures we found on it does not include all the subjects pictured in the Camonica art. But the rock does show a certain number of figures not seen elsewhere; these are, for the moment at least, the only ones of their kind. The rock also contains many figures that are repeated on other rocks and in other regions.

Figures on pages 38 and 39 represent the principal drawings of humans that appear on this rock. Knowing, then, that the other subjects are no less numerous and varied, and that all this material must be classified and analyzed by type before the scenes and compositions can be examined and before we can try to understand their meaning and purpose, it is easy to see the mass of problems we encountered in bringing our study to a successful conclusion.

Conceptually, there are two distinct kinds of pictures: those which are purely descriptive and those which have a symbolic significance. The former, generally representing an action being carried out, do not often seem to have a meaning beyond the scene of which they are a part. The latter, on the contrary, appear as unvaried repetitions, except for lesser differences, of the same figures: for example, human

DISTRIBUTION OF SUBJECTS ON THE GREAT NAQUANE ROCK

	ZONES									
I. HUMAN FIGURES	I	II	III	IV	V	VI	VII	VIII	IX	TOTAL
1. Schematic figure in prayer	2			1	8					11
2. Schematic figure in profile	1				1					2
3. Schematic figure with arms horizontal or lowered	5				3					8
4. Naturalistic figure in prayer	6			1	2	2				11
5. Figure armed with lance	7				11	3	3			24
6. Figure armed with dagger or sword	7	1			5	2				15
7. Figure armed with halberd					2	1				3
8. Figure armed with ax	2				1					3
9. Figure armed with stick	2				4					6
10. Figure armed in some other manner					1					1
11. Figure with objects and tools in hand	12				4	1				17
12. Figure with large hands					5			3		8
13. Figure with ornament	6				2					8
14. Figure on horseback	2	2		1	4					9
15. Praying bust; and other busts	8	1	2	3	16	3		1		34
16. Armless human figures	2				4	2				8
17. Other human figures	1	1				1	1			4
TOTAL	63	5	2	6	73	15	7	1		172
II. ANIMALS										
1. Stags	17	3	2	1	63	10		1		97
2. Ibex or sheep	16			2	14	1				33
3. Dogs	9	2			28				1	40
4. Other four-legged animals	29	1	2	1	70	15		1	1	120
5. Birds and fowl	3				20	2		1		26
6. Fish					1					1
TOTAL	74	6	4	4	196	28		3	2	317
III. BUILDINGS	3				4	6		3		16
IV. LOOMS	7									7
V. LABYRINTHS	2		3		1			1		7
VI. ISOLATED WEAPONS AND TOOLS										
1. Daggers and swords	3	1			3	4				11
2. Axes	8	1			12	1				22
3. Lances			1		3		1			5
4. Halberds	1					1				2
5. Picks	1				2					3
6. Paddle signs	33	3		2	21	1				60
7. Other	10	2		1	11	1				25
TOTAL	56	7	1	3	52	8	1			128
VII. ABSTRACT SIGNS AND GEOMETRIC FIGURES										
1. Footprints					2		2			4
2. Sun symbols and wheels	3		2		4	3			3	15
3. Representations of horns or horned heads	2	1			4				1	8
4. Altars (?)	1				3	1				5
5. Makers's marks	2				3	1	2	1		9
6. Other signs	48	8	8	7	50	11	2		4	138
7. Groups of cup marks	26				24					50
TOTAL	82	9	10	7	90	16	6	1	8	229
TOTAL NUMBER OF CARVINGS IN EACH ZONE	287	27	20	20	415	74	14	9	10	876

Various types of human figures carved on the great Naquane rock.

busts in a praying attitude, paddles, daggers, signs probably symbolizing tools or perhaps abstract ideas whose exact nature escapes us. Usually these are static subjects with abstract meanings and carry a symbolic value in the particular scene. Only after comparative study and a discovery of the laws by which they relate to the other objects in the different compositions and scenes in which they are found, can one finally guess at their significance. This work is, of course, necessary if a conclusion is to be reached; but even the greatest efforts do not always yield results, and many of the carvings are still an inexplicable mystery to us.

4 · The Evolution of Camunian Art

THE STUDY OF STRATIGRAPHY

THE ROCK ART of the Camonica Valley presents different types of carving, alternating schematic and naturalistic, animate and inanimate, designs. The execution of the figures shows enormous variations in technique and workmanship: some are finished works, meticulous and finely chiseled; others have a cruder look. In some, the stippling is consistent over the whole figure; in others, it varies and grows more tenuous at the figure's edges. Still elsewhere, it is superficial and barely visible. In certain engravings only the outline is given; in others, the design's entire surface has been hammered.

Differences are equally apparent in the nature of the scenes and compositions: some groups of signs are evidently symbolic, while others comprise realistic scenes of a narrative character. The form of the weapons and tools pictured develops and changes, as do the architecture of the huts and houses and the manner of their representation.

A study of patinas, of superimposed images, and of the various degrees of wear shows that several typologic and technical phases succeeded each other in the Valley, each with a character of its own. On certain rocks one sees only a single phase. But on others many different types of carving appear, and examination of their stratigraphic relations enables us to establish a chronological table.

One of the most important rocks from this standpoint, and certainly one of the most richly decorated, is the Naquane rock.[1] There we detected fifty cases of superposition, or overlaid images. When one carving belonging to a scene or a composition is covered over by another figure cutting through it, then the whole scene, including the first image, must be considered anterior to the second. This first series of analyses, simple but time-consuming and often requiring very delicate discernment, allowed us to arrange the eight hundred eighty-five figures of this rock in chronological order.

The engravings on this rock represent only a part of the development of Camunian art, but its analysis was the main starting point of Camunian chronology. The facts recorded there were subsequently cross-verified in other rocks, and some of the original suppositions had to be slightly modified. The sequence of stratigraphy was proven to be constant, however, and this was important. The rock showed five main phases which, as it later turned out, correspond to the main subdivisions of late Camunian art, covering phase IIIC and most of period IV.

A series of subsequent analyses resulted in the recogni-

[1] E. Anati: "La grande roche de Naquane," loc. cit.

Table of Periods of Camunian Art

Approximate Dates B.C.	Carving Period	Principal Locations & Rocks	Principal Subjects	Features of Style	External Influences And Main Contacts
?	I New Stone Age (Neolithic)	Rock #1 at Nadro; Pozzi	Sun discs, labyrinths, geometric designs, praying figures	Lack of composition, paired subjects	Mount Bego
2100					
1650	II Copper Age (Chalcolithic)	Boario, Sonico, Scianica, Giadighe, Pozzi, le Sante	Weapons, sun discs, praying figures, paddles, labyrinths, geometrical designs	First attempts at composition	Remedello
1500	(Transition II-III) III Bronze Age Early	Cemmo, Phase I	Groups of animals	Stylized composition; beginning of monumental art	? Aunjetitz
1400	A Middle	Cemmo, Phase II Pasparado	Weapons, animals, suns, maps of fields and houses; plows, war chariots and four-wheeled carts, torques, spiral "spectacle" pendants		I
1200	B	Borno; Rock #3 at Nadro		Monumental art, symbolism, religious scenes	II Mycenae
1000	C Late	Rock #5 at Nadro; Borno		Decline of monumental art; first descriptive scenes	III Terramara
800	D (Transition III-IV)	Caven; Rock #4 at Nadro			Urnfield
	IV Iron Age A Early	Naquane, Seradina, Bedolina	Great variety of scenes; religion, economy, war, houses and villages, animals, weapons, and labyrinths	Complete descriptive scenes	
700	B	Most of the Camunian carvings			
600	C Middle	Seradina, Coren del Valento, Naquane			
550	D	Zurla, North Naquane		Miniatures, meticulous design, perspective; Larger scenes	Nordic (i.e., north of the Alps)
500	E Late	North Naquane		Very large compositions	Greek and Etruscan
250	F				
16	Roman Conquest	Naquane, Bedolina		Degeneration of design and composition	(La Tène) New influence from the north of the Alps, and later, Roman influence

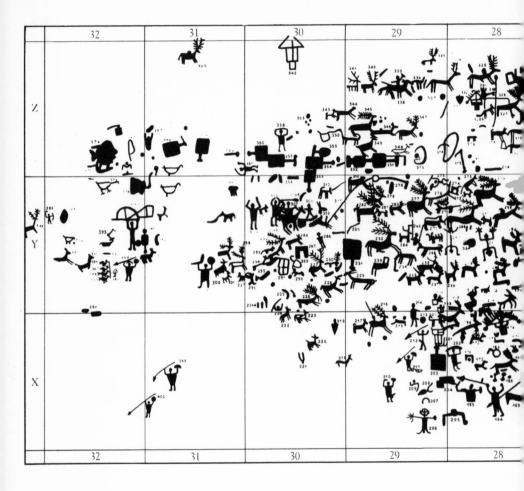

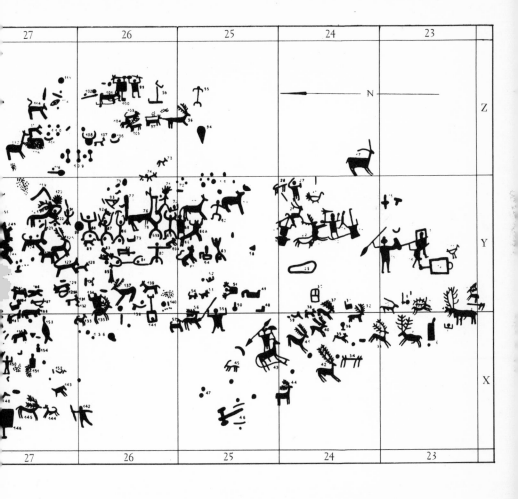

Area V of the great Naquane rock.

45

tion of four main periods in Val Camonica; each is subdivided in turn into several phases, so that we can arrive at a rather clear idea of the stages of Camunian art and of the artistic and cultural changes undergone by the ancient inhabitants of the Camonica Valley.

The last problem before us was that of absolute dating. How old was this art? The carvings often showed weapons, tools, and ornaments which were comparable to objects found in archaeological excavations and whose approximate dates we already knew. It seemed logical to assign to the carvings the dates already determined for objects found elsewhere. This kind of correlation, applied to the different styles, enabled us to establish a chronology for Camunian art.

THE EVOLUTION OF STYLES

THE CAMONICA VALLEY rocks illustrate evolution in the tools and weapons pictured as well as in artistic conceptions and in religious and magic rituals; they allow us to reconstruct patterns of change in the daily economic and social occupa-

Praying figure with sun disc.

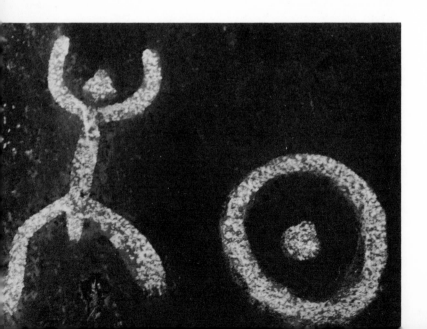

tions of the Camunian peoples. It is apparent, then, that stylistic analysis is extremely important in the pursuit of our study.

Schematic at first, static in expression and symbolic in significance, the Valley's carvings become gradually more naturalistic, more dynamic, and more descriptive. The subjects grow more varied, and the scenes more numerous and complete. Concurrently, the compositional concept undergoes marked transformations. At the beginning, in the first artistic period, the carved subjects are solitary. With all but a few exceptions, scenes and compositions of several subjects are unknown. Most often the picture is limited to a single object or sign apparently unrelated to any other image. Association, where it appears, consists simply of bringing together two or more single subjects; but the only connection one can find among them is symbolic. Their closeness is never conceived with a view to a unified realistic composition in which each subject fills a particular role.

In the second period, however, a new concern with composition comes into being. A remarkable example of this difference appears in the numerous scenes having to do with sun worship. The carvings of the first period are limited to the depiction of one person praying, facing the sun—which is drawn as a disc with a dot in its center.[2] Here the figure of a man represents the group as well as the individual. In the second period the solar disc, now often embellished by rays, is surrounded by several persons in an attitude of prayer or adoration—the worshippers with upraised hands found so often in the Valley carvings. The meaning is the same: this is still the sun cult. But now a man represents no more than

[2] This kind of symbolic representation of the sun is common to many primitive societies and ancient civilizations. It occurs in the ancient Near East, in the Far East, as well as in Europe and elsewhere. It is very common also in the rock pictures of Scandinavia.

47

what he is—one man. To convey the idea of a group, the artist has carved several persons.

This evolution is accompanied by a modification in the technique of incision, which becomes more meticulous and deeper. The carvings dating from the first period are surface work, so light that time has half obliterated them and it is now difficult to recognize the subjects they represent. New carvings sometimes appeared after several days had been spent cleaning off a rock, when we believed that we had found and copied everything on it.

The subjects that seem to have been most frequently treated during the first period are the solar discs we have mentioned, accompanied by worshippers; weapons, especially daggers and axes, often very crudely executed and of a rather limited chronological interest; and finally a multitude of ab-

Thirty-seven praying figures surrounding an ox skull. At lower left, a sorcerer with large hands, wearing ritual costume.

Schematic human figures (man and woman)
from period I.

stract designs somewhat resembling nets or labyrinths, whose
meaning totally escapes interpretation. A growing sense of
composition appears in the next two periods. But the scenes
are very rarely descriptive in character; they almost always
comprise set groupings of signs, tools, or diverse subjects
whose juxtaposition must have been symbolic.

For the most part inert and lacking in organization
during the second period, in the third the compositions gain
sureness; they show stronger purpose and, above all, greater
harmony. The principal subjects of periods II and III are
weapons, animals, plans of fields, and houses. Schematic representations of persons are less common.

Central part of rock III at Nadro, period
IIIB.

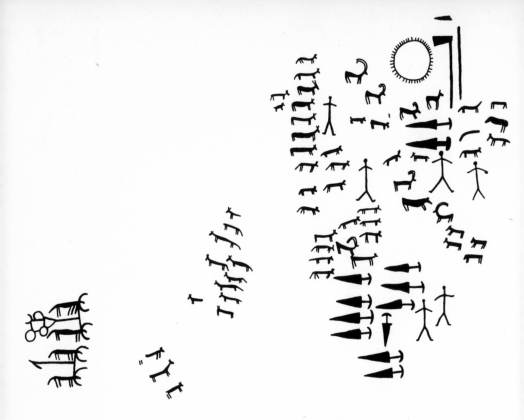

Large composition typical of period III. At left, a four-wheeled cart and plow, each drawn by a pair of oxen. At right, a composition with a solar disc, a halberd, a flat ax, animals, human figures, and daggers with crescent pommels. Second rock at Cemmo.

In the course of the third period one finds a great number of carvings all composed in the same manner and executed with the same technique. The elements of design of these groups are often repeated in the same order in different sites. The pictures of this third period can be divided into two groups of figures different from one another in their conception. The first includes symbolically organized engravings in asymmetrical, monumental compositions. These are generally found on vertical slabs. With the carvings of the second group, Camunian art begins to manifest a certain taste for description; these scenes are always of smaller format, on horizontal slabs, and they often depict religious ceremonies. The conceptual difference between these two groups can be compared with the difference existing today between the frescoes and mosaics decorating churches and still-life and portrait canvases.

In the fourth period, the most richly represented, the scenes reach a high degree of complexity; at the same time they testify to a complete transformation in scene conception. Aside from a few compositions that are still symbolic in character, there are hundreds of lively action scenes. Till period III most of the subjects dealt with in the different compositions had no meaning beyond themselves. Precise as they were, they were also self-sufficient, subordinate to no other figure and dominating none. Henceforth, however, they begin

Human figures from period IV, probably a man and a woman.

51

The Ugo rock at Boario, a typical composition of style II.

to lose their individual value and to derive their sense from a relationship to the total scene in which they appear. Isolated images of objects, weapons, and tools practically disappear; weapons and tools are now accompanied by people who hold them in their hands.

From the technical viewpoint as well, certain characteristics distinguish the carvings of this period from earlier ones. The linear design of the preceding phases, for example, is replaced by people represented in two dimensions, with the entire surface of their bodies dotted. Moreover, the earlier artists used plane projection for subjects whose actual dimensions are rather large, like houses, vehicles, or plows; but in the third period artists often pictured these subjects in both plane projection and front view. These same subjects are drawn exclusively in front view during the fourth period.

The stylistic changes from the third to the fourth period are frequently enormous. A totally different artistic conception appears at this point; and, as we shall see, this fact also reflects very important changes that occurred at the same time in the community's way of life—in its economy, its social structure, and its religion. The contrasts among the first three periods are not so striking; this would seem to indicate that only lesser changes took place in Camunian society during these long centuries.

DATING THE CARVINGS

The problem of dating had already been approached several times by the various archaeologists interested before us in the Valley's engravings. But lack of sufficient data had prevented them from distinguishing the different styles of art and the stages through which it had moved. Given the proximity of the rocks to each other and also their apparent similarity, many scholars tried to group all the pre-Roman carvings into a single period. They had not yet found the axes, daggers, and halberds, for instance, which date from the oldest periods; but they did know the rocks from the third artistic period which bear figures of daggers and other weapons typical of the second millennium. They were also familiar with several Camunian inscriptions written with primitively shaped Etruscan letters which belong to the last centuries before Christ. It is understandable that under these circumstances the carvings could not be dated in an acceptable fashion.

There followed a horde of chronological theories and propositions, none of them agreeing with any other. On the one hand, Professor P. Laviosa-Zambotti claimed that for religious and traditional reasons, fifteenth century implements could still have been depicted in the second century B.C.; on the other hand, it was held that these carvings were no more than a deformation or awkward rendition of weapons from the late Iron Age. Any resemblance to Bronze Age tools was thus coincidental, not intentional.[3] When only the two rocks

[3] P. Laviosa-Zambotti: "Le pietre figurate di Caven in Valtellina," *Atesia Augusta* (1932); cf. id., *Ristagno Culturale e nell'Alto Adige* (1952).

Rhaeto-Etruscan inscription, late style, IX.

Heavy perforated (stone?) ax from Boario, period II.

Dagger with semitriangular blade and round pommel from Boario, period II.

at Cemmo had been discovered, attempts were already made to base chronological conclusions on them—which was taking a chance, to a certain extent, if we consider the meagerness of our knowledge of rock pictures and of Alpine archaeological context in the early thirties. Those two carved rocks, which actually date from the middle Bronze Age, between c. 1500 and c. 1200 B.C.,[4] were in 1930 dated by Professor Marro as from the beginning of the Metal Ages—that is, the start of the second millennium. Two years later, this same author placed them in the Iron Age, or the first millennium.

Raffaello Battaglia, to whom, as to Marro, we owe many important observations on the carvings, and who has con-tributed greatly to their analysis and interpretation, was him-self hindered by an insufficient amount of documentation. Yet it was he who first guessed that the engravings must belong to different ages. Observing that certain weapons and tools pictured were comparable to excavated objects from the be-ginning of the Iron Age, and having also noted the presence of

[4] We refer to the north Italian middle Bronze Age. North of the Alps dates are slightly different; cf.: V. Gordon Childe: *Prehistoric Migrations in Europe* (Cambridge: Harvard University Press; 1951).

56

Detail from rock I at Cemmo, showing
stags and other animals. Time of transition
between period II and III, sixteenth century B.C.

Camunian and Latin inscriptions, he concluded that the carvings had been made during a period stretching from the first Iron Age to modern times.[5] The theory was justified in a certain sense because a few engravings of castles, flags, or crosses are in fact from the Middle Ages. But this small group, which for one thing also includes inscriptions and which appears mainly in the Campanine region, is very different in style and inspiration from the prehistoric carvings. It is extremely difficult to gather everything into a single cycle.

Mme S. Fumagalli correctly demonstrated that the carvings discovered by 1954 ranged *at least* from the late Bronze to the Iron Age; but too little Camunian art had yet been turned up for anyone to undertake its study, and she had found it impossible to establish a valid subdivision. The same problems confronted each of the investigators who in the past few years have tried to evolve a chronology of the Valley's carvings. Other archaeologists tried different approaches based neither on stratigraphy nor on the comparative study of pictured tools, objects, and weapons. Mr. Emanuele Süss, for instance, based his conclusions on the engraving technique, and starting from the wrong assumption that the pictures could have been done only with iron tools,

[5] R. Battaglia: "Ricerche Etnografiche," *Studi Etruschi*, Vol. VIII (Firenze, 1944).

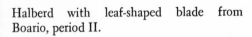

Halberd with leaf-shaped blade from Boario, period II.

Unidentified tool from Boario, period II.

Chronology is determined by the study of superpositions and stratigraphy of the carvings. After each layer is isolated, its components are analyzed to establish the dates of each phase. Here, on the first rock at Cemmo, animals of the transition phase between periods II and III are overlaid by daggers and other weapons of style IIIA.

he concluded that they must belong to the Iron Age. But it was the comparative study of several thousand carvings, starting from their constituent elements, which yielded a worthwhile approach to this aspect of the problem. Once the typologic sequence of the periods and phases of Camunian art had been established, it was possible to attempt a comparison of the objects pictured in the different phases (weapons, tools, ornaments, and such) with those found, together with materials of known dates, in archaeological sites in many regions of north Italy and central Europe. Even though we must occasionally attribute to chance the resemblance between a specific carved figure and some object found in an excavation, there can be little doubt that the whole assemblage of elements in a particular phase of the rock art gives us a reasonably clear idea of the cultural context that surrounds that phase. And this in turn, in relation to what the diggings have revealed, enables us to determine the position of the art phase in a known archaeological period.

We must always keep in mind the possibility of slight discrepancies in time. Some objects might have reached one site a short time before or after the surrounding areas; some elements of material culture may have persisted longer here than there. It is therefore necessary to beware of rigid chronological conclusions. We can, however, check the sequence of

Halberds of style II at Boario, appearing during period II and throughout periods IIIA and B.

material culture in one site by comparing it to that of other areas; and, from the presence of certain elements in a given context, we can establish the level of technology and the archaeological framework represented by the context. With the addition of many other considerations, we can try to propose an absolute dating.

Period I, containing the oldest pictures known at present, is stratigraphically anterior to period II, which is Chalcolithic. Thus it must belong to Neolithic times. We have tentatively dated it in the second half of the third millennium B.C. The designs of the first period, still extremely schematic and some-

Lower part of the second rock at Cemmo. Two human figures at the right, a group of daggers at the center, and a variety of animals at top. Possibly recording a transaction between the two persons represented.

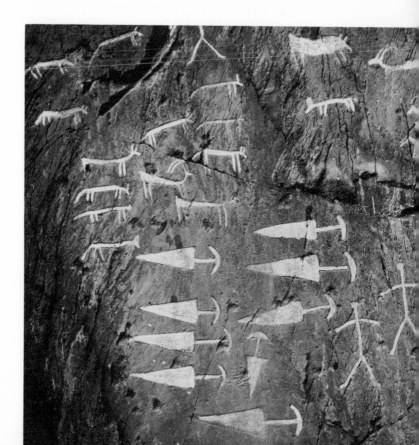

61

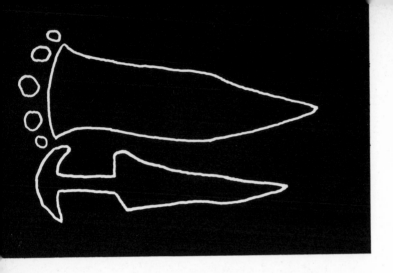

Weapons of style IIIA depicted on the
first rock at Cemmo.

times difficult to read, show mostly implements that seem
to be stone axes and daggers, although neither the form nor
the material of the latter can be clearly made out.

The second period is more distinctive. Certain weapons
appear in it, particularly daggers and halberds, which compare to similar weapons found in the cemeteries of Remedello, Cumarola, Fontanella, Villafranca, and other sites of
the Chalcolithic period in the eastern Po valley. (Italian
archaeologists commonly call that period by the name of its
principal center—the Remedello civilization.) These center-
ribbed Remedellian daggers with subtriangular blades[6] and
round or oval pommels and the halberds with long handles
and elongated blades are extremely important in dating the
second period. This type of halberd is known in the region
and one was recovered in a tomb at Villafranca Veronese; it
shows certain interesting parallels with the halberds that
existed in Iberia at the same time or soon after.

[6] We call subtriangular those blades having a triangular shape with
rounded angles at the handle. This is to distinguish them from triangular
blades with sharp angles.

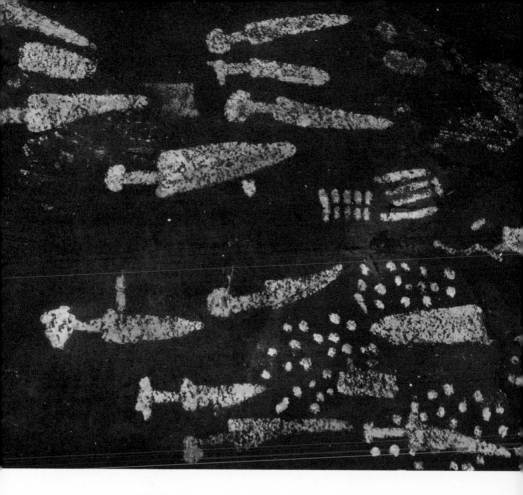

Composition of daggers and dots typical
of period III. Nadro, rock 5, 1200–1000 B.C.

A great many elements of the third period lend themselves to comparison: triangular-bladed daggers with lunate
pommels, necklaces of multiple torques (parallel rings), spiral
"spectacle" pins, and so forth. Several of these are not Italic in
origin; they appear to be borrowings from foreign civilizations.
The dagger with the triangular blade and the lunate pommel,
for instance, is rarely found in the archaeological sites of
north Italy. Yet it is the weapon most often portrayed in the

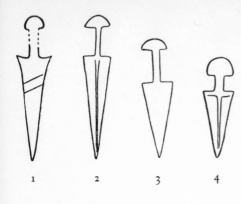

Daggers of the fifteenth and sixteenth centuries B.C.
(1) Mycenaean carving on a funerary stele.
(2) Camunian, period IIIA.
(3 and 4) Daggers carved on menhir statues of the Upper Adige.

Valley between 1650 and 1200 B.C. The triangular shape of the blade, sometimes decorated by a central rib, leaves no doubt as to its age. Similar weapons appeared in Italy for the first time towards the beginning of the Metal Age. This kind of blade, with the half-moon pommel, is best known in Italy from the pictures of it found on the menhir statues in the Upper Adige and in Liguria,[7] and from a little Sardinian dagger in the British Museum. It occurs over a vast area of Europe and is valuable as a landmark in establishing the chronology for period III, for a similar dagger appears on a

[7] R. Battaglia: *Studi Etruschi*, Vol. VII (Firenze, 1933).

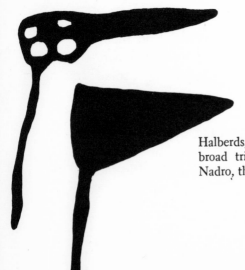

Halberds, one shouldered, the other with broad triangular blade, from period IIIB, Nadro, third rock, 1400-1200 B.C.

64

Mycenaean funerary stele whose age was fixed by Professor Furumark as between 1550 and 1500 B.C. This weapon continues to be the principal one pictured in the Camonica Valley through the first two phases of period III, between 1500 and 1200 B.C.

The halberd seems to have had a long career in the Valley. It appears in period II carvings, with a distinctly archaic character. The same type persists, with a few small changes, into phase IIIA. A new type then appears; its handle is generally shorter, its blade wider and often shouldered. Most typical of phase IIIB (1400-1200), it disappears before the start of IIIC (see the Period Table). A similar type is often encountered in central Europe, where it is associated with a Bronze Age civilization that archaeologists call Aunjetitz, after a typical site of this culture in Bohemia.[8]

It is easy to follow the evolution of the dagger through the three phases of the third period: in phase A the triangular-bladed type with the lunate pommel is almost identical with specimens from Mycenae. Then a change occurs, probably a local one. Characteristic of phase B is a dagger or sword whose blade is shouldered, exactly like certain Greek weapons of approximately the same time.[9] Finally, phase C exhibits a whole array of new types: knives and daggers with blades slightly curved backwards and with rounded, perforated handles—a form widespread in central Europe in the framework of what prehistorians call the Urnfield civilization.[1]

[8] V. Gordon Childe: *The Dawn of European Civilization* (New York: Alfred A. Knopf, Inc.; 1957), pp. 130-2. The similarities with this culture seem to have first reached the Camonica Valley during the late seventeenth or the Sixteenth Century.

[9] According to the Furumark chronology: 1425-1230 B.C.

[1] M. A. Smith: *Zephyrus VII* (Salamanca, 1957), pp. 216-17. This culture derives its name from the custom of its people of incinerating their dead and burying the ashes in urns. It spread over central Europe in the late second

The ring or torque necklaces, which only appear on the rocks together with monumental sun-worship compositions, also supply an important chronological landmark; the torques of the Camonica type belong in fact to the middle and late Bronze Age (1500-1000 B.C.).[2] They are frequent in central Europe and spread as far west as the shores of Portugal, to Scandinavia in the north and Greece to the south. In north Italy they are most often found in the Bronze Age pile dwellings and outstanding specimens have been discovered at Brabbia, Varese, and elsewhere in Lombardy. But in the Camonica Valley the torque collars were pictured throughout the third period.

It is less easy to assign a date to the spiral "spectacle" pendant often depicted in the carvings as well. The problems it raises have not yet been satisfactorily solved. This ornament appears in Europe during the second phase of the Neolithic, in the Danube region. Some scholars suggest that it was brought from there to Troy and Crete several generations

millennium B.C. and introduced into the area highly developed metalwork and many new types of metal weapons and tools; cf. V. Gordon Childe: "The Final Bronze Age in the Near East and in Temperate Europe," *Proceedings of the Prehistoric Society*, Vol. XIV (1948), p. 177ff; C. F. C. Hawkes: "From Bronze Age to Iron Age: Middle Europe, Italy and the North and West," Ibid., p. 196ff.

2 We separate *late Bronze Age* (1200-1000 B.C.) from *transition Bronze to Iron Age* (1000-800 B.C.). See Table of Period, p. 43.

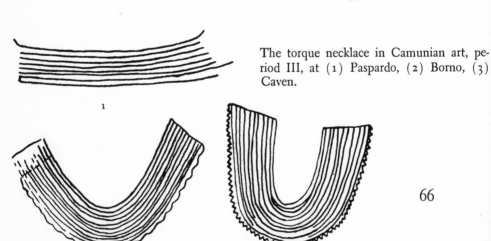

The torque necklace in Camunian art, period III, at (1) Paspardo, (2) Borno, (3) Caven.

1

66

2   3

Central portion of the third rock at Nadro, a rock typical of period IIIB (1400–1200 B.C.). Daggers and swords with triangular (45), semitriangular (31), and shouldered blades (14). (45) is a human figure holding a dagger and a halberd; (34) is a shafted perforated ax.

Menhir statue from Borno showing the headdress of the anthropomorphic statue, eight double-spiral spectacle pendants, symbols of fertility, and one shouldered dagger typical of the middle Bronze Age:

One of the menhir statues from Cave showing a solar symbol with two sets of ra suggesting arms, two circles at the sides the solar disc, and at the right two doub spiral spectacle pendants symbolizing fer¹ ity. Below, a great torque necklace such is often seen in connection with the s god.

later.³ It seems to have been worn through the centuries and into the second millennium, as is indicated by discoveries

³ Very similar pendants occur also in the Near East. In Egypt they appear with the beginning of the Middle Kingdom (2400-1800 B.C.). It is not clear whether a single place of origin should be assigned this pendant in all its areas of distribution.

68

made in central European sites. In the first millennium the pendant, virtually unchanged, seems to have been concentrated especially in two zones: in northern Yugoslavia, mainly in Illyria; and central Italy, on the Adriatic coast, where it is primarily linked to the Picene civilization in the early Iron Age.

Bearing this in mind, I assumed, when I first encountered the pendant in the Camonica Valley, that it belonged to the first Iron Age.[4] But more rigorous examination of its context, and then other discoveries made in the course of our fourth expedition, led me to reconsider that interpretation. The pendant carvings in the Camonica Valley are certainly anterior to the pendant's arrival in central Italy. It already occurs there in periods IIIA and B along with weapons and implements that may be ascribed to the fifteenth through the thirteenth centuries; thus it must be contemporary with them.

Again during phases IIIC and D the Camunian art is enriched by a great number of new picture elements, particularly the lance and the javelin and such defensive weapons as the helmet and the shield. At the same time, the styles and techniques change considerably. In phase D of the third period, the transition phase, there appear representations of knives with curved blades, horned swords (on which antennae or horns rise from the hilt), and countless implements of all kinds. A new era begins: it is the Iron Age.

An important innovation establishes the chronology of the last three phases of the fourth period of the Camonica Valley: it is the alphabet, which appears during phase E (500-250 B.C.), and the primitive inscriptions that employ it. These are still only brief texts and very difficult to date ex-

4 E. Anati: BPI, Vol. LXVI (1957).

actly despite the efforts of several scholars.[5] The characters, in any case, belong to the Rhaeto-Etruscan alphabet. Some of them are still very archaic. These inscriptions coincide with two phases of carvings (*E* and *F*). Phase *E* is very clearly influenced by the Etruscans. The daggers, swords, shields, and helmets pictured in the carvings, and the style of drawing, would place the phase between the early fifth and the early third centuries. That was the period of Etruscan expansion into north Italy. The last phase exhibits, along with inscriptions in Rhaeto-Etruscan characters, two short Latin inscriptions whose characters belong very clearly to early imperial times. Thus, they were engraved around the beginning of our own era.

In the following chapter the reader will see what other perceptible influences and contacts helped us in dating Camunian art more precisely. But this first sketch is sufficient to map the broad lines of its chronology from its birth through its evolution to its disappearance. The material we have described is summarized in the table on page 43.

[5] Cf. F. Altheim and E. Trautmann in "Keltische Felsbilder der Val Camonica," *Mitteilungen des Deutschen Archäologischen Instituts*, Vol. LIX (1939), pp. 1-13.

Human figure armed with a sword and wearing a pointed helmet. Period IV.

71

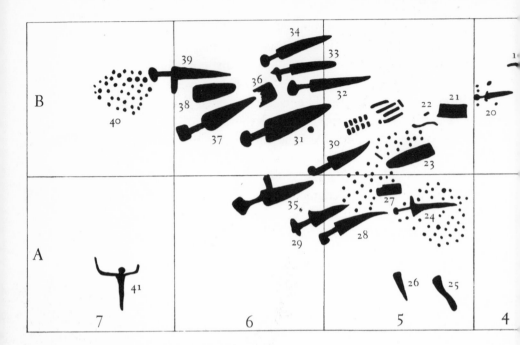

Southern section of rock V at Nadro, a classic rock of period IIIC (1200-1000 B.C.). Daggers of the Urnfield type. At center of segment B 5 is a numerical sign. This rock shows two different kinds of carving techniques, one comprising figures numbered 1 to 13; the other, figures numbered 14 to 40. Figure 41 seems to belong to neither of the two groups.

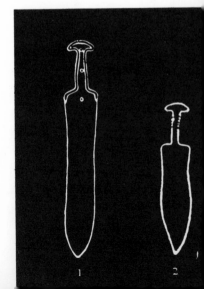

(1) Mycenaean dagger, thirteenth century B.C
(2) Camunian dagger, period IIIB.

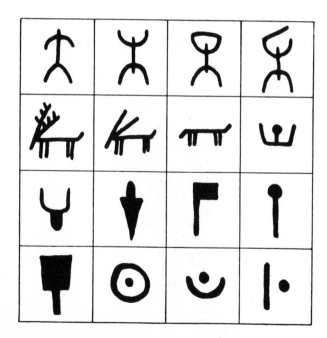

Signs frequently repeated in the symbolic compositions.

ORIGIN AND HISTORY OF CAMUNIAN CIVILIZATION

We see, then, a people till yesterday unknown, bursting suddenly from the dark night of centuries. The Romans called them Camunians, and the residents in the Valley today still bear that name. But who were the first Camunians? Where did they come from? What were their relations with the neighboring populations?

Warrior with shield and spear. Style IV.

The early phase of their art supplies us, as we have seen, with very little information on their origins. The first carvings appear in the late third millennium B.C., probably only shortly after the first carvings of Mount Bego in the French Maritime Alps, which they resemble at the outset. Later they seem rapidly to have acquired their own very distinct character.

This advent of prehistoric Alpine art coincides with a period of great changes in the populations and cultures of contemporary Europe. In the central and western Balkans, the Vinča civilization, probably originating in the Southeast,[6] had been established only shortly before. Central Europe already was occupied by two groups who had brought a new culture with them and whose economy was based primarily on agriculture. One of them, the second Danubian, is divided by archaeologists into two main subgroups—the Tisza and the Lengyel civilizations. The other, which soon spread over a large section of central Europe, gave birth to the Rössen civilization.[7] In the Spanish peninsula the Almería civilization was apparently expanding during the same period, from its birthplace in the southeast to its eventual boundary in the Pyrenees. And finally, there also appeared in southern Italy a new cultural group that Italian archaeologists call Neolithic III or late Neolithic. Soon thereafter the Remedello civilization appeared in the eastern Po valley, and with it the earliest working of metal was introduced into this area. In Austria, Italy, Germany, and Switzerland, villages of so-called pile

---

[6] A. Benac: *Prehistorijsko naselje Nebo i problem Butmirske Kulture* (Ljubljana; 1952).

[7] These various cultures seem to be different localized branches of an agricultural civilization whose common origins are to be found along the Danube river; cf. V. Gordon Childe: *The Danube in Prehistory* (London: Oxford University Press, Inc.; 1929).

dwellings grew up.[8] The most ancient of them, near Lake Neuchâtel, are far earlier than the rock engravings in the Alps. Certain peoples withdrew into the mountains far from the great plains and settled there, retaining for a while a material culture directly related to that of pre-Neolithic times in central Europe and France. As Schlaginhaufen has shown, these peoples were all brachycephalics of the same Alpine race that was later to occupy most of the valleys of the Alps. But it seems clear that the percentage of mesocephalic and dolichocephalic individuals grew greater in time; they were probably imported with the various waves of Mediterranean invaders. By the Metal Ages, this had resulted in a mixed population showing the traits of the two great human groups who then inhabited the region, the Alpine and the Mediterranean races.

Thus, several indigenous European populations, whose technological level was inferior to that of the new arrivals, were progressively driven towards the peripheral, less fertile zones that held little appeal for the more advanced agriculturists. Old bands of semi-nomadic hunters who inhabited the fertile region of eastern Spain were thrust back towards the semidesert zones of the Sierra Morena and the Guadiana basin. Other similar groups penetrated wooded regions like Galicia, the Fontainebleau forest, and today's Luxembourg; and they settled there, where conditions were more favorable for hunting and the raising of livestock than for agriculture.

In central Europe their counterparts filtered across the mountains into the depths of the Alpine valleys, where some of them maintained a cultural level of Mesolithic or archaic

---

[8] In recent years the existence of Neolithic pile dwellings on the Alpine lakes has been much discussed. However, some Bronze Age sites seem to offer evidence that this kind of habitation did exist in northern Italy at that time. Cf. E. Vogt: "Das Pfahlbauproblem," *Monographien zur Urgeschichte und Frühgeschichte der Schweiz*, Vol. XI (Basle, 1955), pp. 119-217.

Neolithic character. It is to these groups that we should most often attribute the rock art of the Metal Ages, and the Camunians probably counted among them.

Certain influences affected them. The nearby Remedello civilization was the first to make an impression on Camunian art. This civilization occupied an eastern section of the Po plain and the valleys along the base of the Alps, in the immediate neighborhood of the Camonica Valley. In the course of period II, the contacts between the two groups were apparently very frequent. They are most strongly indicated in the southern part of the Valley, at Boario, near Lake Iseo. In the north, at Sonico, the same period shows very few implements that could be attributed to the Remedellian.

Later the influence of another population becomes evident—one north of the Alps which became the source of the Aunjetitz culture. In an advanced phase of their culture this group used weapons, halberds especially, similar to those of the Camunians. This is also the moment when the latter make their real entrance into European history—at the beginning of period III in the sixteenth century before Christ.

Since they were forced to settle in a zone that was arid but extremely rich in metals, the Camunians created a metal industry for themselves. Their daggers, halberds, swords, axes —all manner of weapons and tools then in use—achieved a richness and diversity of form until then apparently unequalled anyplace in Europe, with the possible exception of Mount Bego. This activity gave rise to contacts and trade, first with the Remedellians, then with the Upper Adige, and soon after with central Europe and the Aunjetitz civilization.

The middle of the second millennium marks the period of greatest commercial development in the Bronze Age. Minoan Crete and Mycenaean Greece then reached the apex

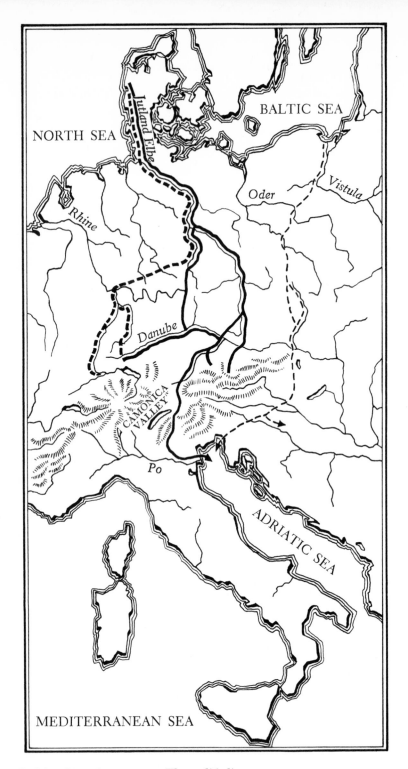

Prehistoric amber routes. The solid lines represent the routes in the early Bronze Age; the heavy dotted lines, the routes in the middle Bronze Age; and the finer dotted line, the route in the early Iron Age.

of their civilizations; their influence began to extend through the Balkans and into central Europe, and shortly thereafter also towards other shores all around the Mediterranean. Commercial exchanges between Greece and northern Europe are evidenced by, among other things, the presence at Knossos and in the Mycenaean royal tombs of amber, then considered one of the most precious of materials.[9] That amber came from Jutland; it was brought to Greece by a route which the British scholar, J. M. de Navarro, was able to map from the remains found along its course in a number of archaeological sites of the period.[1] Leaving Denmark, the amber followed the Elbe river, crossed the Alps near the Camonica Valley, and through the Adige valley reached the mouth of the Po, whence the rest of the trip was made by boat.

We have said that several daggers and spears of Mycenaean type were carved at that time onto the rocks in the Camonica Valley. Moreover, in phase IIIB there are figures of war chariots with two four-spoked wheels, exactly like those found on the stelae of the royal tombs of Mycenae two or three generations earlier and almost identical to those found on the rock pictures in southern Sweden, at Frannarp and elsewhere, one or two generations later.[2]

At Mycenae, in at least one case, a blade was found which belonged to the Camunian type;[3] and in central Europe, at Beitzsch and elsewhere, one encounters war helmets identical

[9] Arthur Evans: *The Palace of Minos* (London: The Macmillan Company; 1921-8) II, p. 170ff.

[1] J. M. de Navarro: "Prehistoric Route Between Northern Europe and Italy Defined by the Amber Trade," *The Geographic Journal*, Vol. LXVI (1925).

[2] Cf. *PPS*, 1960, pp. 50-63.

[3] G. Karo: *Schachtgräber von Mykenai* (München, 1930), pl. XCV-XCVII.

79

with those used at Knossos and at Mycenae.[4] The Camonica Valley, then a metallurgic center, was conveniently situated near the great international amber route. It was doubtless in exchange for its metals that it received manufactured products considered precious at the time, like war chariots and new kinds of weapons.

These material exchanges were certainly accompanied by traffic in ideas; spiritual and intellectual contacts between peoples have always been the great stimulant to progress. And these contacts, as revealed by archaeology, help us to understand the evolution of Europe in the Metal Ages and to see at the same time how civilization spread across the continent. Their study will one day enable us to write the history of prehistoric Europe.

Because of their geographic position, economic organization, and contacts, the Camunian people were in a somewhat different situation from the other contemporary peoples of central Europe whose main economic basis was agriculture; this never had great importance in the Camunian Valley. Until the Roman era, the Camunian people always remained hunters and miners. Nevertheless, the material culture of the Valley continued to parallel the development of neighboring societies, though the other groups were entirely based on agriculture. At the end of the Bronze Age, Camunian culture scarcely differed from that of the other peoples of central Europe. Later we will have occasion to demonstrate that this was also true in religion and partly true in social organization.

The connections between Camunian art and the art of the Upper Adige during period III are interestingly shown by a group of statue menhirs in the neighborhood of Bolzano. In fact, this group is rich in representations of torque necklaces, axes, halberds, daggers, and such, just like the Ca-

[4] H. Hencken: "Beitzisch and Knossos," *PPS*, XVIII (1952), p. 36.

War chariot of Mycenaean type from Naquane.

munian rocks in the third period.[5] Triangular-bladed daggers with moon-shaped pommels, characteristic of the Camunian style, are also found there. These daggers, incidentally, present one of the most interesting problems of the period. (See illustrations, pp. 61-64, 100)

We know that they were widely used in Mesopotamia in the third millennium; the excavations in the royal cemetery at Ur have revealed some remarkable specimens. Towards the end of the third millennium they appear in Syria, at Ugarit, at Alalakh. Shortly thereafter, at the beginning of the Middle Kingdom, they occur in Egypt, where their image enters into the composition of the hieroglyphics;[6] and in Anatolia, where they seem to arrive at the beginning of the Hittite empire. Mycenae, around 1700 B.C., marks them with its own style.[7]

[5] M. O. Acanfora: Le statue antropomorfe dell'Alto Adige (Bolzano, 1953).

[6] A. H. Gardiner: Egyptian Grammar (London: Oxford University Press, Inc.; 1911).

[7] A. Furumark: The Chronology of Mycenaean Pottery, (Stockholm, 1941), p. 94.

Finally, in the course of the seventeenth century, they appear in the Camonica Valley, where they are portrayed on the rocks for a long time afterwards. It was probably in the same general period that they reached England; the Stonehenge carvings show some beautiful pictures of them.[8] The true significance of this diffusion still escapes us; what is certain is that this dagger, whose picture is found over so vast an area, had acquired a symbolic and religious value, that it originated in the Orient, and that it was considered an object of worship. The Camunians and some other Alpine peoples accorded it actual veneration.

Toward the end of the second millennium the Camunians seem to have had a steady relationship for the first time with some populations of southern Germany, France, Switzerland, and Austria—the people of the Urnfield civilization, probably ancestors of the people later given the collective name of Celts.

Toward the beginning of the first millennium the appearance in our carvings of antennae swords, of lances, shields, and helmets, and of new types of vehicles indicates the relations that apparently existed between the inhabitants of the Valley and the late Urnfield civilization, which at the time spread across parts of what is now Austria, southern Germany, and northern Italy.

Then great changes occur in central Europe: civilizations disappear, others are born and develop. The map of European prehistory is in the process of transformation. But in the Camonica Valley the population, withdrawn into itself, seems out of reach of these great blending movements; it holds to its traditions, continues its hard-working life, and goes on carving its rocks. The new weapons of the times, and

[8] Cf. O. G. S. Crawford: "The Symbols Carved on Stonehenge," *Antiquity*, 109 (1954), p. 25ff.

especially the great technical discoveries like ironworking, bring a little variety with them. Actually, however, we observe no radical change; there is simply an enrichment of the designs and an increase in their number, along with a new artistic style and a broadening of the gamut of subject matter. All this took place during the transition period, which lasted two hundred years, and there is nothing to indicate any abrupt and drastic variation. On the contrary, despite the new cultural elements, the basic customs remain the same, the economic foundation has undergone but little transformation, society is still organized on the same bases, and the population obviously has not changed.

After that date, and all through the Iron Age, outside influences make themselves felt more strongly and more frequently. A cultural wave from north of the Alps, which Altheim calls Celtic[1] and which appears in the early sixth century, is succeeded by a slow but very noticeable Italic surge from the south. At the time the Camonica Valley lay at the frontiers of the Etruscan empire; and countless Tuscan elements can be recognized in the carvings that range from the sixth to the third centuries. Arms, implements, even clothing arrive in the Valley from Etruria. The style of the Camunian artists reflects the influence, and it is not hard to find parallels between the works they carved at the time and more sophisticated decorations found in the bronzes and frescoes at Cerveteri and Tarquinia.

The Celts do not arrive on the scene until the Iron Age. Originally they were tribes of various backgrounds who spoke a language of Indo-European basis enriched by many local additions. Thus, it seems to me more correct to speak of a

[1] F. Altheim and E. Trautmann: "Nordische und Italische Felsbildkunst," *Welt als Geschichte*, Vol. III (1937), p. 83.

Celtic civilization than of a Celtic people. This cultural group formed on the outer rim of the Alps; the Camunians found themselves more or less gathered into it. When the Celtic La Tène civilization appears, the Camunians are part of it, and so the observer can follow the trail by which Celtic culture gradually infiltrates into the Valley with no simultaneous change in the population. Thus, we can trace the different phases of Camunian history from the moment it enters the orbit of the Urnfield civilization. The evolution was slow. Everything seems to indicate that it came about through cultural contributions of the neighboring civilizations, rather than through ethnic changes.[2]

Once the Camunian people arrive at this stage in their history, they begin a long decline. Their rough and simple art turns to other avenues. A concern with effect and the imitation of forms and subjects borrowed from the outside soon rob it of that marvelous awareness and feeling for the raw rock and of the sense of direct contact with nature which for fifteen centuries had tied man to stone and had given the Valley civilization its special and unique character.

At the time when Europe was seeing the rise of powerful expanding civilizations like that of the Gauls, the Ligurians, the Celts, or the Etruscans in the south, when through their influence the peoples of the continent were tending to seek cultural and economic unification, the population of the Camonica Valley felt itself powerless to stanch the tide advancing on it from every side. Already its autonomy was no more than a memory. Rome's hour had come. For yet an-

---

[2] The present considerations concerning the Camonica Valley should not lead to the conclusion that an identical cultural process took place everywhere. In areas where Celtic civilization made its appearance far from the Alps, such as Brittany and Ireland, the problem is totally different and must be examined separately.

other brief instant the Camonica Valley was to remain within the sphere of influence of the north, but the future mistress of the world was already the stronger. The Latin spirit was incompatible with the old Camunian civilization, with its introversion, its conservatism, its obsolescense. New ideas, a new mentality, a new economic and social structure were to deal it the death blow. Evidently the principles which had given it birth were no longer able to resist new and stronger values. Spiritually, materially, the old mountain tribes had fallen apart. In changing, in modernizing, the principles would favor the assimilation of the Alpine barbarians by the Roman Republic, and their eventual integration into the Empire.

Rome's extension of her hegemony over that part of Cisalpine Gaul, the implanting of her administrative system there, was for the Camonica Valley the end of a long evolution, the inevitable result of a more and more headlong decadence. Camunian art had already ceased to exist, and, probably at the same time, so had the social organization of the country by clans and tribes. The imperial administrators could take the place of local chieftains, the Roman deities could be set up in the sanctuaries of the old gods. Henceforth, instead of the primitive village huts there would rise small houses of stone and mortar; the stony mountain trails would be abandoned for broad flagged roads. The frontiers that had immured the Camunians in their hideaway would be broken down, and with the same surge, modern life would penetrate to the farthest corner of their lost land. The narrow Alpine valley that had managed to keep its independence and all its characteristics for two millennia, the tiny sovereign state, submitted to engulfment by the Empire and accepted her new identity as no more than a remote canton in a faraway province. How could her population have resisted the

85

armies of Rome, when morally it had already been conquered by its terrible neighbor?

The occupation of the Valley was accomplished with little effort. One day during the year 16 B.C. the legions of Publius Silus entered Oglio Valley.[3] The last rock carvings must date from about that time. On the rocks they cover are found the two short Latin inscriptions mentioned before, traced in the letters of the Augustan century.

Strabo and Pliny mention the Camunians in passing. The first calls them Rhaetians; the second, Euganeans. But neither tells us much about them.[4] For these authors, as for the soldiers who conquered them or the administrators named to rule them, the Camunians were simply a handful of half-savage mountain folk to whom Rome was bringing civilization. Their name figures often in the lists of vanquished Cisalpine tribes. But there is almost total silence on their religion, their art, their way of life. The rare authors who give them any attention at all view them simply as a detached branch of the Celtic tribes of central Europe.

Under the new organization, the Valley's principal center was probably at or near the village that still bears the name of Cividate Camuno. The prehistoric carved rocks are plentiful in that area: several later, Roman, inscriptions were also found there.[5]

History has nonetheless preserved one last trace of the Camunians' existence; their name may still be read on Augustus' trophy at La Turbie, among those of the other conquered peoples. Thus closes the last link of the chain. The Metal Age, with its free and primitive peoples, flows into the

---

[3] Dion Chrysostom: LVI, 20; Pliny: *Natural History*, III, 24.
[4] Strabo: IV, 6, 8; Pliny: *Natural History*, III, 134.
[5] *Corpus inscr. lat.*, v. 4954, etc.

Empire and is swallowed up in it. Central Europe moves into history, but for many centuries, till the end of the Middle Ages, it will be night and the return to prehistory in the Camonica Valley.

5 · The Rock Engravings: Their Composition and the Scenes They Depict

ANALYTIC METHODS

THE ARCHAEOLOGIST who undertakes to study Camunian art finds himself confronted with an array of lines and designs crowded so closely together that they mesh almost inextricably, or else actually lie one on top of another in undecipherable patterns. Rarely do we find groups of carvings readily legible, sharing the same technique, or executed by the same hand. The observer's problem is to discover the relation of each figure to the others. To solve it where different styles and techniques are mixed together, he must isolate the various strata for later study, each in its own context. Then the

88

figures fall into small comparable groups, in which the same subject often reappears.

In many cases it is not difficult to see what the artist tried to represent; for instance, the persons who stand with weapon in hand, facing an animal, are obviously hunters. Men face to face, with swords, are warriors fighting each other; the groups of praying men, gathered about a god or his symbol, are worshippers in a cult.

On the other hand, it is frequently very hard to decide how certain subjects should be grouped. In some cases the relationship between carvings is much more obscure; for example, in the always identical signs engraved on broad surfaces during the schematic periods, which are so close together that it is practically impossible to determine when one

Area II of the great Naquane rock, showing carvings from three different periods.

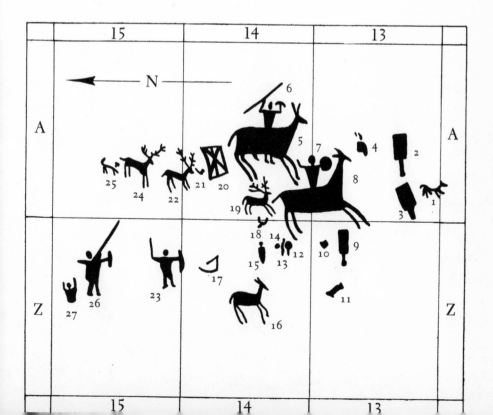

War scene from area II of the great Naquane rock with carvings from other periods eliminated. Compare with illustration on p. 89.

Hunting scene.

ends and the other starts or which of the pictures is related to others and which is an entity in itself.

The detailed study of more than fifteen thousand carvings eventually enabled us to recognize the mentalities of the artists of different periods, their customary methods of grouping several subjects in the same scene, and finally the diversified styles they practiced in the innumerable repetitions of the same scenes. This helped to dispose of a certain number of questionable cases.

Nevertheless, a very great number of carvings were never deciphered; the task required defining the relations of the different subjects among themselves, and in many cases we were not yet even able to determine which ones, in a scene or a whole grouping, were meant to be related. In these compositions, naturalistic scenes of a descriptive character—episodes of war, hunting, fishing, other renderings of the daily life of the inhabitants—occur together with a mass of figures which apparently represent neither a situation nor an action. Their arrangement never seems to suggest a logical connection between one sign and another. Quite often one senses a symbolic meaning to the carvings—the objects they picture could also represent an action, in an abstract form. For instance, the shapes indicating a dagger, an animal, an altar, a person in prayer, the sun, or a slaughtered animal are rather easy to read. But the abstract significance of their interrelation might not be understood.

It is not a simple thing, for example, to interpret the frequent iconographic sequence of the bust of a worshipper, a paddle, and an animal (see page 92). There are hundreds of such cases. All we can say is that these are signs of very definite form and that they are intentionally repeated in the same manner. It is certain, however, that they must have represented something, despite the stylization and simplification

Compositions with symbolic signs.

Symbolic compositions with paddle figures.
Each design constitutes a symbol which
appears in several compositions.

which prevent us from relating them to anything we know.

These signs are often gathered into groups of three to seven, mostly on the same line, like the words of a sentence. There is reason to think that they represent not some kind of game of graphic repetition but a primitive attempt at the expression of a thought. Each sign must have the value of an idea. Thus, we confront the most extreme form of picture symbolism.

Elsewhere, peoples who had reached that stage of symbolic iconography went on to invent writing. Many primitive communities, at different times, drew near to this major invention without ever pushing on over the threshold. Consider, for instance, the schematic designs that cover the stones of the Mas-d'Azil (though this interpretation is currently under fire) and the designs dating from the metal age which have been found in Andalusía, in the Negev, and in other areas where rock engravings flourished. Highly conventional kinds of symbolic designs were also used in Pre-Columbian America by different peoples, and the same principle is still current today among certain Eskimo tribes.[1] It is probably correct to say that the symbolic compositions of the Camonica Valley are a process of expression rather close to ideogrammic writing. Its similarity to the early Egyptian and Minoan hieroglyphics is striking in any case, even though the system appears in fact to have gone no further than a crude beginning. The most frequent signs number only fifteen; they are the most abstract. A few others, more naturalistic in appearance, occur less frequently; and some are unique. The most common signs must have had specific meaning and were probably used as basic reading terms. The idea to be ex-

[1] F. G. Mallery: "Picture Writing of the American Indians," *Annual Report of the Smithsonian Institution* (Bureau of Ethnology, Washington; 1888-9).

Symbolic compositions with signs having
numerical value.

pressed crystallized around them. They seem to have signified
an action. Did they represent the central idea, the verb of the
sentence? Most of the time their schematic nature rules out
any possibility of interpretation.

The other signs occur occasionally in different forms and
seem to depend mainly on the imagination and the fancy of
the engraver. Possibly they stand for the subjects and objects
of those ideogrammic sentences. They usually show persons,
animals, or divine symbols (the solar disc, for example) set
one beside the other. Clearly, this system limited the possibility of expressing several ideas at a time.

Signs made up of lines and dots may have indicated a numerical value. The great Naquane rock bears about a hundred such designs. We show the principal ones on page 96. They are repeated, as they are on other rocks.

Harder to decipher is a carving of the Nadro area—two lines, one above the other, each composed of five dots and four vertical bars, somewhat similar to the numerical signs of the Minoans and other ancient peoples. It could well be that they are figures and numbers, although at the moment this cannot be proved. And even if this supposition turned out to be correct, the material we have so far is unfortunately too meager for us to determine the number system the Camunians used. Looking at the Nadro signs and some others of its kind, all we can say is that it was not the decimal system.

Lastly, the carvings include a kind of abstract figure that is not found in the symbolic compositions; these figures are conventional signs that recur often and always in the same form. They generally appear in naturalistic and descriptive

Scene of sun worship. A sun with rays and a spirit beside it, surrounded by praying figures.

scenes; their position is always the same, in the lower part of the engraving or at the side. It was a long while before we arrived at any understanding of their meaning. The presence of these signs near certain scenes had struck us from the outset of our work. We had also noted their repetition and their similarity. That they belonged to the scenes near which they were found we never doubted, because the technique of their execution was identical to that of the rest of the composition; but we could not understand the presence of these abstractions in the midst of naturalistic scenes.

Finally, however, by comparing them with other signs sometimes rather similar in nature, whose meaning we know, we have perhaps succeeded in unraveling the mystery. The Bedouins of western Asia, for example, use certain signs in this manner to mark and recognize their petroglyphs and the animals that belong to them, particularly their camels.[2] The use of these brands, which they call *wassum*, is very old; it goes back at least to the first millennium B.C. There are *wassum* cut on the petroglyphs of the Negev, and some of them are much earlier than the arrival of the Romans in the region.[3] Each tribe has its own mark; the custom makes it possible to know who owns the animals in a herd. They are sometimes called property signs. In the desert they also serve to denote the owner of a well.

In an analogous area, we are familiar with so-called potter's marks. These are the tiny signs made on ancient ceramics,

[2] H. Field: "Camel Brands and Graffiti," *Supplement to the Journal of the American Oriental Society*, Vol. XV (1952).

[3] E. Anati: "Rock Engravings from the Jebel Ideid," *Palestine Exploration Quarterly* (London, 1956).

Numerical symbols of unknown value on the great Naquane rock (row at left) and at Nadro (center).

particularly those from the Near East, and were probably the trademarks of the workshops that made them.

Thus, we can reasonably assume that the signs in the Camonica Valley, to which we eventually gave the name of maker's marks, can be similarly explained. They must be a kind of signature, probably not the artist's own but rather that of the tribe or clan to which he belonged. The signs are doubtless a mark of the group and not of an individual. The fact that they are most often found beside carvings of animals or of herds would seem to indicate that the Camunians, like the Bedouins, used them to identify their cattle as well.

But the signs present many other problems that have not yet been solved. So we shall abandon the study of these abstractions now, curious and interesting though they are, to examine instead the naturalistic figures; for it is in them that the Camunian artist best reveals both his nature and his mind.

THE CAMUNIAN ARTIST

It was probably only after long and painful groping that the primitive artists left the elementary stage of pure and simple design for the higher one of the scene. The step assumes a certain artistic progress and above all an intellectual one. The representation of an object demands no more than an awareness of the real and an application of attention to reproducing directly that which presents itself to view. Descriptive scenes, however, presuppose a complex, abstract thought process able to make associations, able to conceive and organize an action. They also demonstrate their author's capacity to relate the represented subjects among themselves, either logically or symbolically. Before the discovery of Camunian art we could study the successive stages of this development in two principal regions: in Spain, where they are most clearly defined, and in Sweden and Norway. The Camonica Valley provides a third example. In these three regions, the development took place at different times, and in different ways.

In eastern Spain the Levantine art cycle shows the process best. In its earliest phases this art contains naturalistic animal figures. At Albarracín, La Minateda, and the other sites where they appear, each figure is at first depicted in isolation. Several animals may be depicted on the same wall, but they show no signs of belonging to complex scenes. In later phases we follow the slow process of association. The animal figures become part of hunting scenes in which men take an increasingly prominent part. The static isolated figure acquires dynamism, and action is depicted. The dates of these various phases are still very much debated, but whatever they are, this art represents a way of life economically based on hunting and gathering. Thus, in terms of European archaeology, this means a cultural level preceding the Neolithic Age.*

In the southern Scandinavian cycle things happen in a different way. In the earliest phases we meet with abstract symbols rather than naturalistic figures. These symbols slowly acquire realistic forms and organize themselves into logical assemblages. The transition probably occurred during Neolithic times, but the figurative approach remained for a long time, with very primeval concepts of composition. It is not until the late Bronze Age that the first real scenes appear.[4]

In the Camonica Valley the findings do not so far permit the precise determination of all the steps between the primitive stage of simple design and the more advanced stage of descriptive scenes: the most ancient specimen of Camunian

* E. Anati, "Quelques réflections sur l'art rupestre d'Europe." *Bull. Soc. Pré-hist. Franc.*, LVII (Paris, 1960) No. 11-12, pp. 692-712.

[4] This material is currently under study, and it will be possible to say much more about it soon.

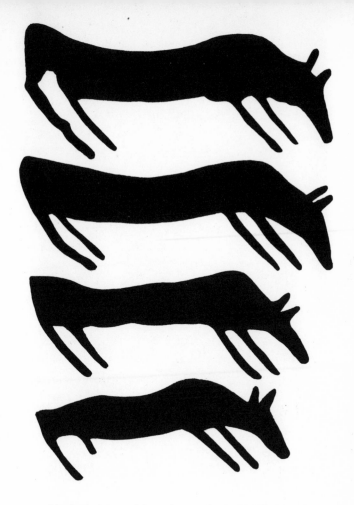

Typical composition from the transition
period between II and III, Cemmo, rock I.

art known shows already, in a rather consistent manner, a
start in the association of ideas. It is not uncommon to find
subjects and symbols which complete each other—for example, a person in an attitude of adoration and, before him, the
disc of the sun; or a paddle and the solar disc; or an ax and a
worshipper together. From the second period onward, large
static compositions appear. Scenes, properly speaking, are
difficult to find, since the drawings do not generally record an

Rock of the five daggers at Paspardo, ex-
emplifying the abstract composition of period III.

action caught in the moment of its happening; these would
sooner be described as situations. Static, idealized, they exist
outside of time. Often they are, for instance, groups of people
in the conventional position of prayer and adoration. As many
as thirty-eight of these worshippers have been counted on one
of the Naquane rocks; they cover a surface of more than four
square yards. Though scene is not quite the word to define

such a grouping, what the observer sees is nonetheless a composition already founded on some notions of harmony and balance.

The sense of composition, already rather advanced at this stage in the artistic development of the Valley, appears primarily in large patterns composed solely of lines, dots, and dotted surfaces; these are maps of fields and villages, as certain more naturalistic carvings of later periods have taught us. But not till period III does composition reach its highest level. The greatest development of the statue menhirs in northern Italy and in France took place then. These monuments, as we have pointed out, show numerous points of similarity to the carvings of the Camonica Valley's third period. They indicate that an artistic sense comparable to that of the Camunian artists existed in a great many regions of central Europe at the time.

In the third period, examples of harmonious composition are numerous; looking for instance at the animals carved on a rock at Cemmo and on the rock of the daggers at Paspardo—among the most beautiful—it is evident that each element plays its role in the whole. Crowded as they are, the different subjects do not touch one another. One might speak of a regular asymmetry; for never does the composition show symmetry of form, and there is no regular repetition of the same figures. At Paspardo two daggers are carved in front of three; at Borno the solar disc that constitutes the principal subject of a certain composition appears at the side of the carving rather than at the center. The two spiral "spectacle" pendants near it are also placed asymmetrically. This does not preclude each figure's having its place and its own value in the composition, however. The esthetic sense manifested here—whether conscious or not—is nonetheless sure.

The Camunian art of the third period occurs either as

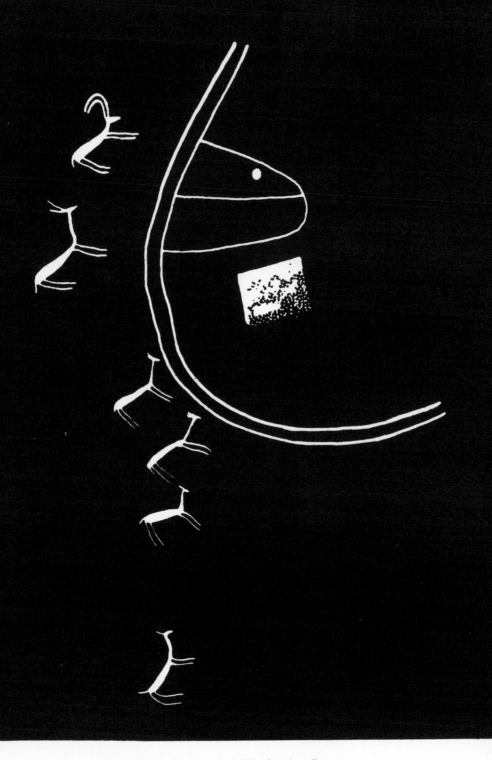

Composition from period III, showing ibex running toward the river, from the Borno rock.

monumental religious art whose symbolic compositions, sometimes repeating themselves in similar fashion, cover vertical
slabs of sizeable dimensions; or, more modestly, as descriptive
art. Much smaller in area, the descriptive scenes are engraved
on horizontal slabs. Here for the first time the action is caught
at the very moment of its play and in all its complexity. Nothing like it exists either in earlier periods or in the monumental
art of this period. Realism now makes its appearance.

To execute these scenes, the artists used a linear technique; everything is reduced to line. But soon, toward the end
of the third period, the transformation becomes even more
radical: a new dimension intervenes. The earlier stylization
tends to disappear, and at the same time the awkward rigidity
of the subjects yields to a taste for movement. The scenes
take on rhythm; life begins to stir in the carvings. Man is no
longer represented simply in the conventional and static
gesture of prayer; now the artist knows how to make him
execute the most complex actions, and give him the most
varied positions—in fact is able to show him in the whole
range of his daily activities; hunting, at war, in his workshop,
at his plow, building his house. It is a veritable revolution in
art. Prayer and religious ritual no longer provide the sole and
elementary subjects of inspiration: the reproduction of events
and of a multiplicity of everyday activities becomes the purpose of the carvings. Composition is sometimes affected; it
is less fastidious, less harmonious. For the new style has yet
to find its rules, its rhythm, and all its possibilities. It is still
feeling its way.

The sense of the real and the observing spirit which the
Camunian artists evince during the last phases of period III
lead them as well to discover the rules of perspective, for
which maps and abstract projections had substituted until the
end of the Bronze Age. Vehicles, swing plows, and houses are

Cart from period IVC. Note attempt at perspective and rendering of horses' galloping movement.

drawn full front; huts and their roofs are sometimes in three-quarter view; the size of the animals, under the yoke that couples them, varies according to their position in relation to the observer; so do the diameter of the wagon wheels and the distance between them. There are amusing details, like hut staircases that turn back on themselves. It is a veritable artistic renaissance. In any terms it is an almost total abandonment of the abstract and symbolic conception of the Bronze Age; Camunian art is meeting with reality. The first investigations in this direction had already appeared several centuries earlier in one of the most common subjects—a subject which, for its purpose, demanded complete conformity to reality: maps of fields and villages, which occur in great number. From the manner in which houses, garden walls, granaries, wells, paths, and other details are represented, one gathers that they are copied from reality. And this was certainly the case. In this respect, two maps of the Valley are particularly astounding. The first, discovered by Raffaello Battaglia, shows the Valley cut in two by the Oglio river, and on its banks here and there cultivated fields separated by little walls.[5] The other,

[5] R. Battaglia: "Ricerche Etnografiche," *Studi Etruschi*, Vol. VIII (1934), p. 15.

discovered in the region of Bedolina, represents the landscape of the valley as seen from the very spot where it was found; it is a true map of the region.[6] Even the Rè, a small creek that runs down from the mountains, is traced with meanderings very like those it follows today. It is all there except for certain separating walls between the different fields which are no longer where they were three thousand years ago when the prehistoric artist had them before his eyes as he chiseled. The photographs we reproduce show both the rocks with the carved map and the landscape of the Valley as it looks from this spot (see pp. 106-8).

It is easy to see that artists of the European Bronze Age had a sure sense of the real.

THE MEANING OF THE SCENES

Much has been written on the significance of rock art and of the carvings on statue menhirs. These are usually described as a religious expression, but scholars have not often attempted to carry their research much further, nor to explain the deeper meaning or the purpose of this prehistoric art. Although occasionally the statue menhirs, or some of them, can be connected with the death cult, what has so far been written on the religious meaning of rock-carved art is still in the realm of speculation. Nowhere has material been found that would indicate, through its association with the carvings, the kind of cult to which they are related. Even the assertion that rock pictures are a religious expression cannot be supported in all cases, though it has been repeated so often as to have become a kind of axiom in the field of prehistory. I think, for instance, of the art of eastern Spain. What does one find there? Hunt-

[6] E. Anati: *Archaeology*, Vol. XI (1958), p. 36.

The Bedolina rock. Below, village houses with human figures. The central house seems to be built on stilts. Above, cultivated fields, streams, and canals.

The same rock seen as part of the actual
landscape today.

ing scenes and war scenes, others showing the honey harvest, persons running and other details of daily life. What explanation can be given for these scenes? If they do have religious significance, what is it? The situation is the same in the Camonica Valley, where the rocks abound in scenes of a narrative character, plans of fields, erotic pictures, and descriptions of battles, some of which seem to derive from concerns other than religious ones. Many pictures of course have a religious meaning, but which ones? For what religious purpose were they executed? With what cult were they connected? Here as elsewhere the carvings raise questions that often remain unanswered.

Two problems present themselves to the student seeking to understand the significance of a prehistoric engraving: first, to try to discover what it represents; then, to attempt to determine its *raison d'être*, to say why it was made. The first can often be resolved; the second is far more difficult. Consider, for example, a carving quite frequent in the Camonica Valley, one with a solar disc and a human figure in prayer. The meaning is self-evident: here is a person praying before the sun. But ask anything more about it and complications arise. Why was the design made? For precisely what purpose? Did the artist have a particular reason for executing it? The answer is not easy. We can hazard a few guesses, but certainties are lacking. For some scholars the scene would seem to represent a rite of initiation; for others, a propitiatory act; and for still others, a magic ritual. We shall have occasion to return to this subject.

Let us examine the general pattern of the evolution of Camunian art. If we can explain the reasons for the changes it underwent, we shall have some interesting ethnological and psychological material. Camunian rock art, as we have seen, is comprised of abstract and symbolic works and of works of a descriptive character. In the first group are included the monumental compositions, so classified because of their dimensions and the arrangement of the subjects treated. Their subjects are found in other abstract composition; we shall discuss them again later. For the moment it is enough to know that they are the solar disc, the stag, the dagger, and the praying figure. Each has a definite religious significance that we shall study later in more detail. These figures are extremely numerous during periods II and III, but they disappear in the course of period IV. At the same time the subject matter, which in the third period had been solely religious in nature, becomes considerably more varied; and from period III to period IV the repertory of the carvings grows progressively richer. There are fewer engravings of a religious character and more and more representing the daily occupations of the Valley's inhabitants. A greater importance is also granted the different realms of life and thought. The monumental art disappears at the end of the third period. In the carvings of religious character in period IV, one finds mainly mythological persons, spirits and imaginary beings, whose advent probably indicates a degeneration in the archaic religion and shows a considerable change in the psychology and spiritual values of the people. The conventional religion of the Bronze Age has given way to a world peopled with spirits of all kinds. Such magical beliefs characterize the European Iron Age and occur in various European countries in different kinds of cultural groups. Some of the fantastic half-human figures in these rock pictures are comparable to figures which decorate Iron Age tools and objects in various European countries. Others seem to have been prototypes of images in Teutonic mythology. The enrichment of iconography seems to indicate a new interest in life in general, in the different daily occupations, and in the objects of common use which had had no attention until now.

The laicization of art, which led it to discover the world and turn further and further from its religious preoccupation, clearly shows that a profound change is taking place at the time in the minds of the Valley's inhabitants. When I mentioned this transformation in Camunian art, a visiting local archaeologist said to me: "At that period man moved out of the earthly paradise; he became conscious of himself and felt responsible for his own destiny. With a will and a resolution which could never again be braked or stopped, he set about climbing out of the abyss where he had vegetated for centuries and undertook his long march towards the peaks of civilization and of thought." Despite the somewhat romantic tone of this statement, there is undeniably some truth in it. Figurative art illustrates this clearly; the change in its subject matter *is* an expression of changes in thought and civilization. The abandonment of ritual scenes of contemplation and adoration in favor of scenes taken from life seems to indicate that from this date forward man, till then the plaything of divine caprice, decided to take over his own destiny, rather than confide it to the inhabitants of the heavens.

The scenes of religious inspiration did not vanish entirely; they continued to be graven alongside the realistic scenes. But they were fated to hold a lesser place from then on. Another remarkable effect of this evolution, to which we shall refer again, is the progressive transformation of deities into human form, whereas previously they had appeared in the form of inanimate objects or animals. The change is more than a change in the subject matter of rock pictures. It is a change in the attitude of man towards himself.

6 · The Economic Foundations

AGRICULTURE

THICK WITH FOREST, overgrown by a vegetation often so dense that walking through it is nearly impossible, the slopes of the Valley have nonetheless retained traces of the ancient populations that occupied them long ago; and it is not unusual to find, among the thick brush or the crumbled leaf mold, the remains of terraces or boundary walls from a time when the Valley was the center of a rather advanced agricultural life. These dry-stone structures very probably date from the last few centuries before the arrival of the Roman armies.

At that time the cultivated areas stretched to the hillsides. Because certain parts of the plain must have been swampy, the peasants passed them up for the heights. But lakes and bogs probably filled only a few of the deeper spots. We have proof that different parts of the Valley must have been under tillage for a long while, at least from the middle of the second millennium B.C. Certain carvings from period III, only some twenty-five feet above the present level of the Oglio river, near the village of Capo di Ponte, lead us to believe that at one time almost the whole Valley was dry in that area. The Bronze Age maps of which we have spoken, the one cut on the Bedolina rock and others discovered in the neighborhoods of Seradina, Bedolina, Pozzi, and Giadighe, offer irrefutable evidence of this. On them are small plots, planted evenly, with an occasional well in the center or in one of the corners. Walls separate the fields, and the wells supply dozens of canals that branch through the land. Aerial photographs of the Valley give the impression that the creek, the Rè, has changed its course several times, and they also show traces of old stoneworks which could well be the remains of prehistoric diversion dams.

From the vestiges of terracing left on the ground by the ancient tillers of the Valley, one can deduce that the agriculture they practiced had advanced beyond primitive methods. The fields covered dozens of acres. This strongly suggests that they were maintained by clans or tribes and that such works as canal construction were probably executed by groups through mutual agreement. The canals, in view of their strictly planned declivities and of the distances the networks had to run to water or to drain the vast plantings of the Valley, could only have been the result of a long-term program established by general agreement. Even their construction must have been the result of collective labor.

Certain fields were reserved for the raising of domestic animals, but most of them were devoted to crops. According to the Bedolina rock, there were at least four kinds of produce; in the carvings each kind is indicated in a different manner, by dots or other signs of a definite shape and dimension. But it

Pair of oxen drawing a four-wheeled wagon.
Style IIIA-B.

Bronze Age plow drawn by two oxen, from
Cemmo.

is impossible, for the moment, to tell what these crops were. The most we can assume, if our interpretation is correct, is that fruit trees held an important place.

The carvings also give us information on the implements used in working the fields; the swing plow and the pick. The latter was often constructed in two pieces—a handle and a pointed head. It was held with two hands. The diggers, who often worked in groups, walked behind the swing plow. It was probably used to open and turn the earth, and the large chunks it raised were then chopped into small pieces or crumbled by the picks. Very widely and commonly used from the third period on, the swing plow was probably already known in period II, as two figures of that time seem to attest. Until the middle of the Iron Age, it was drawn by two oxen coupled in a single yoke. Only two carvings exist showing a swing plow pulled by horses; they date from the late Iron Age.

These swing plows, of a rather simple type called a spade plow, were just like those used by farmers in the Alps today to work the earth on the mountainsides. The plow consisted of two main parts: an axis that attached the instrument to the yoke; and the body of the instrument, fashioned into a helve at one end and into a sole or slade at the other. Only a single example of a hoe plow has so far been discovered; the picture was found at Seradina in a carefully wrought scene of phase

Development in the representation of the plow. Periods II, III, and IV.

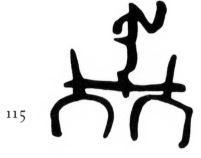

115

1

2

3

Tentative reconstruction of the pick frequently seen in rock pictures, a wooden pick made of two pieces.

IVC and thus dates from the sixth century B.C. This hoe was pulled across the field; the moldboard acted as a sole and the handle took the place of a beam. These two types of plow also appear in the rock carvings at Mount Bego in the Maritime Alps, and in Scandinavia. But in the Metal Age the spade plow seems to have been more commonly in use than the hoe plow everywhere. Interesting comparisons can be made between the carved representations and the vestiges of plows found in peat bogs or in other archaeological sites. Professor Glob has made fundamental studies of those discovered in northern Europe.[1]

[1] P. V. Glob: "Ard og Plov i Nordens Oldtid," (Aarhus, 1951).

Farming scene showing persons cultivating behind a plow. At the bottom, an artist's sign. Between the two animals, an ox skull.

The picture we can reconstruct of rural life in the Camonica Valley in the prehistoric period, based on these two types of representation—maps of fields and agricultural work scenes—is of course quite vague. We know nothing, actually, of the nature of the crops, or of the system utilized by the primitive farmers of the Valley to fertilize their land so that they were able to cultivate it for centuries without exhausting it. A rudimentary agriculture already existed at the time that the Valley carvings abandoned their old abstract style, and everything indicates that later, at the end of the Iron Age and especially in Roman times, agriculture had reached a level of expansion far superior to that known in the Valley today.[2] But we do not know how this advanced agriculture came to the region how it developed, what it was at the onset, or what it later became when it reached the intensity that the carvings and the remains of agricultural walls indicate. The rest is even more obscure. What can we say, for example, about the system of organized labor that must have been practiced and of the agrarian collectivism suggested by the construction of plot walls and irrigation canals? Again we are reduced to speculation; the rare documents available provide no more than a general notion of a system that appears to have been quite complex.[3]

If we examine the carvings in the Valley which show an economic character, we observe that agriculture occupies the

[2] In fact, remains of ancient terracing are found in areas that are today totally invaded by woods and bushes.

[3] As we shall see, despite the fact that there must have been a communal work system to prepare the land, the private granaries pictured near many houses seem to indicate the private ownership of agricultural products.

Farming scene at Seradina. A plow drawn by two animals, followed by a woman cultivating the ground, with a child on her back?

117

Plan of a village, with square buildings,
paths, and people. Late period III.

third place in importance; hunting scenes are much more
plentiful. Handicrafts, or scenes that imply them, are also
better represented. On the great Naquane rock, for example,
there are forty-four hunting scenes, five scenes related to animal raising, four depicting handicrafts, and only one scene of
agriculture and one of fishing. In the Pistunsi zone, at Bedolina, the proportion is lower: only eighteen hunting scenes as
opposed to eight of agriculture and two of livestock farming.
Although we have not yet been able to formulate definitive
statistics for all the rocks studied and for all periods of Camunian art, the impression is that agricultural scenes multiply
with the centuries, becoming very frequent with the beginning
of phase IVC. But they never become more numerous than
the carvings dedicated to hunting.

HUNTING

Hunting constitutes an essential theme of many scenes of economic, religious, and magic nature. Wild animals and their capture did indeed occupy an important position in the religion of the Camunians. The proportion of symbolic compositions relating to the magic of the chase gives one to suppose that this activity formed one of the principal bases of Camunian economy and that it played a large role in ritual and thought. This is a male occupation par excellence, and it is not infrequent to find human figures with exaggerated muscles and powerful weapons near the hunted game.

Stag hunting is the most usual; it figures in more than three quarters of the carvings. The others record the pursuit of large wild animals, generally of the goat or fox families. Some carvings also show the capture of aquatic and marsh birds, which must have abounded in the Valley; in the Iron Age many species had been domesticated by the inhabitants.

The bow and arrow were not very commonly used by the Camunians; they preferred the sword, the dagger, the spear, the ax, and the halberd. But since these weapons are somewhat impractical for hunting, they must often have captured animals with the snares found pictured on the rocks. Of

Scenes of lance hunting. At left, the man is aided by a dog. At right, the man wears a ritual headdress.

Carrying wild game?

the forty-four hunting scenes on the Naquane rock, thirty show the trap and the net in use. In the other fourteen the hunters are using their usual weapon.[4]

There were four different kinds of snare. The first trapped the animals by the paws. As far as one can judge from the simplistic representations, this method is comparable to that still employed today in northern Italy to capture rabbits or hares. It consists of an open noose laid flat on the ground and tied to a flexible branch which is bent and held taut in this position. When the animal treads on the snare, he releases the branch, which snaps up suddenly, tugging the rope with it and tightening the slipknot at its end. The carvings, obviously, do not show the successive steps in the operation, only the result. We are therefore reduced to conjecture as to how, exactly, the snare worked.

4 E. Anati: "La grande roche de Naquane," loc. cit.

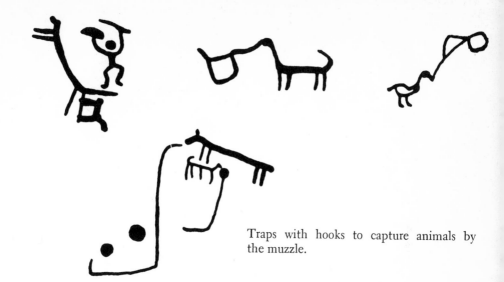

Traps with hooks to capture animals by the muzzle.

A second style of trap caught the animals by the muzzle; this must have been a kind of baited hook. Like the first type, this one seems to have been used primarily for smaller animals. Large animals required a vaster and apparently much more complex arrangement: a trap into which the game was attracted; once in, it could not get out again. Close examination of the carvings gives the impression that this snare was made up of many parts, which the artists, doubtless fascinated by the complicated mechanism set into motion, tried to reproduce.

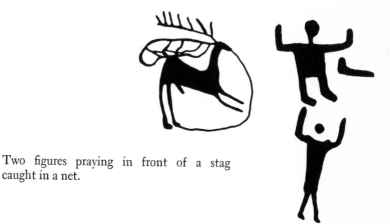

Two figures praying in front of a stag caught in a net.

Hunting with a net. At right, a schematic praying figure in front of three objects: a paddle, a schematic net, and an unidentifiable third object.

Nets were also used. In one carving, quite naturalistic in style, a stag is the victim. This trap was probably used in the woods, then, like the slipnoose, and stretched behind a tree.

In all the engravings the animal, at the moment he is captured or after, is surrounded by a pack of dogs. Several carvings show packs in pursuit of herds of stag and of other wild game. They must have been trained to drive the prey through the fields or forests toward the traps.

For hunting birds there were two main types of snare. One caught them by the beak; it was set on the ground and probably resembled the one used for capturing small animals —perhaps a hook attached to a string. The other is difficult to determine, for very few details are given in the carvings; but

Dog facing a stag.

Stags caught in snares.

it seems to have been useful in catching ducks and other water birds. One of the carvings on the Naquane rock contains a long-necked bird, possibly a swan, whose feet are not drawn; this suggests that it is being shown in the water. Near it stands a person who holds in his hand some complicated object, which the engraver detailed minutely. The object was very likely a snare of the second type.

Once the animals were caught in the trap, the watching hunters approached and killed them with spears or axes. Hunting with war weapons was not very common. Still, the Camunians did sometimes use the lance and the *cateia*. The lance, from the start of the Iron Age, was their favorite

Band of stags pursued by dogs.

123

weapon. Its strength, and above all its accuracy, made it a good hunting weapon. Of fourteen figures showing armed hunting on the great rock at Naquane, nine portray hunters equipped with lances; three, hunters armed with *cateia*; and two show men carrying unidentifiable weapons.

The *cateia*, according to Latin writers, was a weapon used among the Celts. It was, it seems, a kind of ax with a light, flexible helve, a foot and a half or two feet long. "If it is well thrown," says Osidorus, "it will return to him who flung it." Thus, in principle, it recalls the Australian boomerang. In the *Aeneid* Virgil tells us that the *cateia* also served as a war weapon.[5] Although the *cateia* does not seem to have been very commonly used in the Camonica Valley, it is pictured occasionally on the rocks. In the three carvings on the great rock we have mentioned, it occurs once in the hand of a hunter and twice in the back of a stag. Here it has the appearance of an ax with a short handle and a long head. But scenes showing animals killed by a spear are more frequent.

Camunian hunters did not work alone but in pairs. This was doubtlessly necessary to finish off big game and to carry it back to the village.

A great quantity of documentation is available to us on the Valley's game: mainly stags, foxes, ibex, wild boar, and some forest rodents. From all indications, there were also wild felines, such as lynx and cats; all kinds of birds; and fish. The Camunians evidently hunted all these, but their preference was for the stag. Thousands of carvings are devoted to its pursuit; very likely it formed the basis of the Valley's economy.

[5] *Æneid*, VII, 741.

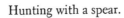
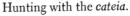

Hunting with a spear.   Hunting with the *cateia*.

A series of inscriptions from period IVF
associated with drawings. The hut at upper
left, center, is overlaid by the outline of
a footprint from a later period.

One curious, and still unexplained, fact: 88.3 per cent of
the animals pictured on the great rock at Naquane face
south. The rock lies parallel to the Valley, running north-
south in direction. Only thirty-eight animals have their bodies
turned to the north—that is, toward the mountains—while
two hundred seventy-nine are shown running southward,
toward the plain. Among the animals facing north are fourteen domestic dogs. Ten animals are depicted as trapped; two

are birds, and four are domesticated goats.[6] Only eight are clearly wild beasts at liberty, heading back to the mountains. Although we do not yet have such precise statistics on the other rocks, we would probably find as high a percentage of wild animals moving southward. What conclusion can we draw from this? The first explanation that comes to mind is that in the Metal Ages, the plain was inhabited rather densely and evenly. The wild animals must have chosen to live in the woods, on the northern heights. Thus, from the viewpoint of the Camunians, north was the direction from which game appeared.

A natural corridor rimmed by high mountains, most of them difficult to traverse, the Camonica Valley was crossed by many herds of wild animals in migration. The inhabitants knew their trails and seasons and must have waited for them to pass. Moreover, we can be fairly certain that, when the weather grew harsh, animals from the peaks would come down to the pasturelands of the plain to find food. The slopes of the Valley must have provided an ideal natural reserve all through the Age of Metals, even as it does today. In that mountainous region rich in thick forests, stags and chamois still abound. This was a windfall to the population, who thus had an inexhaustible source of food within hand's reach.

The well-favored situation of the Valley made the Camunians a hunting people; and they remained such until the Roman epoch. Hunting was more natural and more familiar to them than agriculture; in a sense it was thrust upon them. They had only to train the dogs and set up the snares. Their whole civilization reflects this fact.

---

[6] We can tell wild from domesticated animals by studying the scene in which they appear. In hunting scenes the animals are either dogs at the service of the hunter or wild animals, while in herding scenes they are domestic.

STOCK FARMING AND DOMESTICATION

A shepherd with animals gathered about him—this is the Camunian artist's description of the raising of livestock. The shepherd is recognizable, within the conventions of the carvings, by the pole he carries.

Stock farming, we have said, was less common than hunting. Of the three hundred seventeen animals pictured on the great rock at Naquane, eighty are domesticated and one hundred seventy are wild; we have not been able to classify the other sixty-seven. Some idea of the importance of stockbreeding in comparison to hunting, in the Camunian economy, can be gained from the fact that on this same rock only five scenes are devoted to stockbreeding, while forty-four portray the hunt.[7]

[7] I would like to warn the reader about these percentages. They probably give a precise idea of the interest of the Camunians in various occupations, but they do not necessarily inform us about percentages of time and working hands devoted to these tasks. We must keep in mind that the interest aroused by various occupations is not, and has never been, the direct consequence of their economic value. In the present case, hunting was not only an economic occupation but also a source of male expression, and the interest devoted to it was probably much greater than warranted by economic need.

Herdsman at center of his flock. In upper part of the scene, an artist's sign.

Sexual perversion.

Dogs, goats, sheep, oxen, horses, poultry, and pigs formed most of the farm population. Dogs were very numerous—a species with a large head and erect ears and tail. They were used primarily for hunting and are often seen in the carvings rushing in pursuit of stags or other wild animals. They also helped shepherds to tend their flocks. Each family had its own dogs, and the engravers took great care, when they drew villages, to show them guarding houses or playing before huts. Dog bones frequently uncovered in prehistoric excavations in Europe have already demonstrated the position this animal held among Metal Age peoples. The Camunian carvings provide supplementary evidence.[8]

[8] Max Hilzheimer, "Dogs," Antiquity, Vol. VI (1932), pp. 411ff.

Horses and oxen were used principally as means of loco-
motion or transport; but they were much fewer than the dogs
or the cattle bred for food. Oxen appear in the carvings from
the second period of Camunian art (2100-1650 B.C.); the yoke
does not appear till the end of this period, but it becomes
more common in the course of succeeding centuries. Towards
the end of the Bronze Age, in the transition phase between
periods III and IV (1000-800 B.C.), the horse is included on
a broad scale for the first time. Up to this point we know so
far of only one drawing of horses; it shows two of the animals
hitched to a Mycenaean war chariot (phase IIIB: 1400-1200
B.C.). No horseman is astride them until the seventh century.
Before then they occur only rarely on the rocks; the animal
must scarcely have been used in the Camonica Valley, and

Raising geese.

then mostly as a display animal. Only chieftains or war heroes seem to have owned them. Horses apparently became more frequent in the sixth century, since two thirds of the pictures we have of them were carved between the sixth and the first centuries before Christ. Doubtless an imported item, the horse must have come in numbers to Camonica Valley at the same time as the first influence of the Hallstatt Iron Age civilization.

The review of what we know of animal farming among the Camunians will be completed with the mention of the great quantity of ducks, geese, and such, which probably played and swam in the ponds and marshes of the area; of the goats and sheep; and of the pigs, whose presence is indicated in only one scene found so far belonging to period IV. Though only slightly developed, stock farming was sufficient, along with hunting, to fill the needs of the population; it provided them with such food as meat, milk, and eggs and with the organic materials indispensable to their small industries, such as leather, hair, wool, horn, and bone. In addition, the animal excrement probably fertilized their soil.

FISHING

To date we know of only five pictures of fish in the Camonica Valley—three in the Boario region, on a rock that juts over the Valley and must at one time have overhung a small lake, one in the Pistunsi region and two others on two rocks at Naquane. They occur in fishing scenes. At Boario the fish are pictured inside a grillwork formed of parallel lines—a kind of schematized net or pot well known to ethnologists. These

Fish in a net, from Boario. Style II.

nets, made of two or three progressively smaller meshes and usually woven of vines or another flexible vegetable fiber, are set across the water current; they imprison the fish that enter them. They are still used today by primitive populations in certain areas of the world. A similar net is to be found in some regions of the Alps; it resembles a kind of rushwork basket that allows the fish to enter but not to escape.

Although the Boario carvings are excessively schematic, it is still possible to recognize a net of this same type. The round and very stylized fish that appears on the great rock at Naquane is also in a trap, but one whose shape is somewhat unclear. In front of the fish there is a hatchet: might it symbolize the fate that awaits him? On another rock at Naquane (rock 50), we see a fisherman in the act of capturing a fish with a harpoon. But the numerous superpositions that have covered the design in later periods make its reading very difficult. The fisherman seems to have horns on his head and to hold a large object in his other hand. The image and the relations between man and fish are not clear.

Another very interesting carving on that same rock represents a person in a little boat shaped like a half-moon, and recalls the prehistoric carvings of Sweden.[9] But the dimensions

[9] A. Fredsjo, S. Janson, C. A. Moberg: *Hallristningar i Sverge* (Stockholm, 1956), p. 116, fig. 42.

The round fish of Naquane. Late period IV.

131

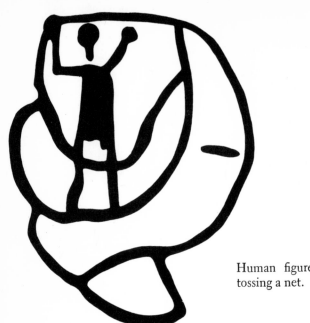

Human figure in a small boat, probably tossing a net.

of the Camunian boat are much smaller. The fisherman has thrown an object into the water and keeps one of its ends in his hand. The object, asymmetrical in appearance, is tied to the boat by a short rope. Mr. Mafessoli thinks it may be a net, which is very possible; the fishermen of the area still use nets of a somewhat similar type. Once in the water, the nets take on a conical shape and close at the mouth when the fisherman pulls on the rope.

The carvings at Boario showing snares go back to the Chalcolithic age, between 2100 and 1650 B.C. Those at Naquane and at Pistunsi are more recent; they belong to the late Iron Age and date from the late first millennium. Fortunately, they are quite clearly cut and provide us with information on fishing techniques, but there are very few of them. The relatively unimportant rank of this activity in Camunian art must correspond to reality; fishing was probably no more than a minor added contribution to the economy of the Valley.

HANDICRAFTS

To gain some idea of what life must have been centuries ago in the Camonica Valley, one should go into the small villages clinging to its slopes today. The modern Camunians continue the work of their ancestors—stockbreeding, farming, hunting—in the rhythm ruled by the seasons, with the same gestures and sometimes with the same tools. Life hardly seems to have changed in three thousand years, and the villages strangely resemble those in the carvings. Without electricity, until recently without roads, the inhabitants live outside the world as unaware of them as they are of it. Horses and wagons are still the only known means of transportation. The influence of the priest just barely balances the power of the sorceress, to whom the villagers still appeal in time of need or sickness. Each rock perpetuates ancient legends and ancient superstitions. It is as though time had stopped, for after civilization marched into the Valley with the Roman legions, the old culture survived in the surrounding woods and mountains. The people themselves are conscious of this. The fertile and well-cultivated valley where highways run and factories have sprouted constitutes a mysterious and faraway universe in their eyes—almost another planet, whose inhabitants have discarded the old traditions for a mentality and mode of life that scandalizes the old folk and tantalizes the envious young.

The ancient social categories have survived, and in these peasant hamlets the blacksmith, the carpenter, the shoemaker, the merchant form a class apart. They have neither farm nor field; they never hunt. Their workshop is their kingdom. In exchange for their services or for the products they make and sell, they are often given not money but flour, poultry, and hides. The craftsmen are privileged in the villages; they be-

133

Work at the smithy. See comments on this
scene on p. 135.

long to the elite. They are richer than the peasants and usually
work less. Honor and respect are theirs. The mayor is often
chosen from this class; and so are the men delegated to represent the community at regional gatherings in the plain.

In the pre-Roman world, particularly among the Celts,
craftsmen enjoyed the same privileged status. The richness
of their tombs offers incontestable proof: one of the most
opulent tombs known from the Iron Age is that of a blacksmith.[1]

Handicrafts were well developed among the Camunians
of prehistory. The carvings afford us valuable evidence of their
diffusion and importance during the Metal Ages, especially

[1] Paul Jacobsthal: *Early Celtic Art* (London: Oxford University Press,
Inc.; 1944).

the Iron Age, in the first millennium before our times, when the highest point of development was achieved. Innumerable scenes show metalworking, weaving, lumbering, the building of carts and plows. Often information on other occupations, such as mining, the manufacture of idols for religious worship, and the making of traps and nets, is also indirectly provided in the carvings.

Blacksmith wearing a ritual headdress.

We have found a certain number of engravings that describe the working of metal; usually no more is depicted than the smith at his forge. But occasionally there are amusing, picturesque details. In one carving, for example, aside from the smith and his helper, or apprentice, there is another man and an animal. The Abbé Breuil, to whom we showed it, thinks that it tells a story. The man at the left might be a hunter; the animal he wants to capture is represented symbolically at the top of the composition, above him. But the weapon he needs to use, which lies in front of him, is broken in two. So he takes the pieces to the smithy, as the movement of his legs indicates. He gives the broken weapon to the apprentice; the boy in turn will hand it to his master, who will repair it. The engraving is a kind of cartoon strip. It is probably correct to interpret in the same fashion other anecdotal scenes discovered on the Valley's rocks, when they thus lend themselves to explanation by picturesque tales.

Inside a blacksmith shop.

Another forge scene discovered by Professor Battaglia is also very interesting to study. We see, inside a little house, a person at a forge on which he seems to be working a tool with his hammer. Outside are two objects attached to a rope. Signor Battaglia thought that this might be a ventilation system for the forge. This scene is extremely late, dating back to the last phase of the last period of Camunian art.

The very many pictures of arms and implements found on the rocks leave no doubt at all as to the importance of metalwork in the Valley. The diversity and the wealth of these weapons and tools also postulate the existence of a real industry. In fact, there is every reason to believe that metalworking formed an appreciable source of revenue for the Camunians; as we have seen in one of the preceding chapters, they did engage in export to neighboring countries. The soil of the Valley today is still very rich in metals of all kinds, and metal industries in Breno, Boario, Costa Volpino, Pisogne, and

Person with ax. Lumbering or woodworking?

Laverne form a vital part of modern Italian economy. Silver, copper, and iron are abundant; the veins almost burst through the soil's surface. Until the start of this century, development of the region's mines was in the hands of a few families and a few small workers' groups. It is only very recently that work came to an end in most of these small mines; in a few, work was undertaken on an industrial scale. But today still, in some sites, certain methods of extraction are the same as in the pre-Roman period. The indications are that some of these mines were already being worked in prehistoric centuries and that from them the Camunians obtained raw materials for their local industry.

Constructing a hut. Two people are working inside. The roof is not yet finished.

Lumbering was no less highly developed. The Camonica Valley was surrounded on every side by thick forest, and the people we see in the carvings with ax in hand are doubtless the first woodsmen of those antique forests. In primitive in-

Scene probably showing the building or repairing of a hut. A man is working on the roof.

137

dustry wood held an important role: it served in the construction of houses and entered into the fabrication of weapons and tools, of wagons, plows, and boats, of traps and nets.

The building of houses is described by a whole series of carvings; in one we see people lifting a heavy beam onto a roof whose framework is not yet complete. Another carving, showing someone beating iron on his anvil with a heavy mallet, represents the construction of a cart. The wheels and the axle, at the feet of the blacksmith, are already finished. To build a wagon, the collaboration of the smith and the carpenter was solicited; this is still true in several villages of the region. The cartwright must have been an accomplished specialist because at that time the cart was by far the most difficult and complicated of structures.

The weaver's work is described on the great rock at Naquane in four scenes in which seven looms appear. In one scene four persons, in pairs, carry two looms on their shoulders. Actually, we cannot say exactly what they are doing. As in other analogous carvings, the person whose arms are empty and who stands before the working figures must represent the proprietor. In certain symbolic compositions this figure seems

Two people symmetrically depicted inside a building. Middle period IV.

The making of a wheeled vehicle. The wheels and the axle are ready near the craftsman.

Two looms being transported, one framed
by paddle signs.

to take on an ideographic value and mean "me" or "mine."
Here there are two such figures, each standing before one of
the looms being transported.

A carving which shows two men—one holding an animal,
the other an implement probably meant for spinning or weaving
—and above them a loom, probably summarizes the principal
operations of the wool industry, from the fleecing to the spinning and weaving. In two of these four carvings the artist has
drawn two looms, one beside the other. This detail is extremely

interesting: it reveals the existence of a weaving industry developed beyond a simple domestic craft. In two scenes we see persons busy working at a loom; others, beside them, watch and seem to direct the work. Another carving which includes seven persons altogether shows two couples at work.

All the looms in the Camunian carvings are similar; the model represented is always the same, only its size varies. In every case it is an upright loom, very simple in design, without leash, based on the principle of weights to hold the warp threads in position. Other examples of this type of loom are known from the Metal Ages. The model was common in Egypt beginning as early as predynastic times.[2] Upright, weight looms like those in the Camonica Valley are also pictured, beginning at least in the seventh century, on some Greek vases.[3] Another example is found in a painting on a Hallstatt vase of the tenth century from Ödenburg.[4] The Polish archaeologist J. Kostrzowski[5] has succeeded in reconstructing one from debris. The result is startling: the antique Polish loom is no different from the ones used in the Camonica Valley. The type, then, was very common in Europe from

[2] Brunton and Caton-Thompson: *The Badarian Civilization* (London: British School of Archaeology in Egypt; 1928).

[3] C. Singer and others: *History of Technology,* Vol. I (London: Oxford University Press, Inc.; 1956).

[4] S. Galley, in *Archaeologia Hungarica,* Vol. 13 (Budapest; 1938).

[5] J. Kostrzowski: *Wielkopolskaw Pradziejach* (Warsaw; 1955).

Weaving scene, with two looms and a person working at one of them. In the center, a paddle sign.

the Metal Ages on; but the carvings of it in the Valley are, at least for the time being, the most ancient pictures of it known in central Europe.[6]

The interest of prehistoric peoples in weaving is well known. An art of adornment, a feminine art, it had considerable importance. Mythology offers further evidence of this. The industry was put under the protection of female divinities —Neith in Egypt, Athena in Greece. Homer speaks of it with admiration and returns to the theme many times, in reference to Queen Arete and to Penelope. In German mythology, cloth weaving had the goddesses Freya, Frigg, and Holda as its patronesses. It is obvious that the occupation played an enormous role in the life of women of the Metal Ages. This must certainly have been true in the Camunian society.

The Camonica Valley was thus particularly favored. If industry was able to reach a rather remarkable level of advancement, as the carvings indicate, it is because the raw materials necessary were all there: copper, silver, and iron in the mines; wood in the forests for the construction of houses and the making of carts and tools. There was more than enough to allow this people to live and grow. Nature was indeed generous to them; but they too deserve credit for their enterprise and intelligence.

TRANSPORTATION

The Camunians used three means of conveyance: the saddle horse and the wagon on the ground, the boat on the river and on the ponds. We know only one, rather late, specimen of their boats; it has been described on pages 131-2.

[6] They belong to period IIIC, thus to 1200-1000 B.C.

The Valley carvings, on the other hand, have left us plentiful and highly interesting documentation on the wagons, enough to allow a rather accurate retracing of their whole history. The first wagons appear towards the middle of the second millennium. They were still light harness carts on four wheels and were probably meant to be pulled by two animals, although in the carvings of the period the carts are generally shown without them. Later, in period IIIC, they are more frequently harnessed to pairs of oxen. All the carvings we know show paired beasts in harness, and this is true up and into the Roman period. The Camunians seem never to have used more than two beasts of burden for their wagons, despite the considerable increase in the weight of the loads observable after the end of the second millennium.

Oxen were used at first. The domestic horse appeared in the Camonica Valley toward the end of the second millennium but did not come into popular use until the beginning of the first millennium, during the transition period from the Bronze Age to the Iron Age (1000-800 B.C.). Before that date the horse appears only once in the carvings, in a picture of a war chariot imported from Mycenae which we have already mentioned.

The Iron Age left behind it in the Valley countless pictures of wheeled wagons, some of which must have been splendid. They are generally much longer than those of preceding centuries and are hitched to horses as often as to oxen or asses. Their wheels have between four and eight spokes; they are practically the same as all Iron Age vehicles whose remains or pictures have been found in Europe. Their resemblance to the famous prehistoric wagon recovered in the marshlands at Dejbjerg, in Jutland, is striking; those of period IV also recall a type of wagon whose design appears on potsherds discovered at Ödenburg, in Hungary, and in other

Pair of oxen drawing a four-wheeled wagon.
Style IIIA-B.

sites of the Hallstatt Iron Age civilization.[7] Wagons maintained practically the same form throughout the Iron Age.

In many carvings from the fourth period in which figures of wagons occur, they are followed or surrounded by persons engaged in prayer. On one of them a funerary urn is being carried. This same kind of cart is depicted on a statue menhir at Lagundo in the Upper Adige. It is likely that these vehicles are intended for a particular function—probably the death cult, as we shall have occasion to demonstrate later.

[7] Cf. W. La Baume: "Bildliche Darstellungen auf Ostgermanischen Tongefässen der Frühen Eisenzeit," *IPEK* (1928), pp. 25-56.

Mules yoked to a cart. Transition III-IV or
very beginning of style IV.

The four-wheeled cart of the Camonica Valley seems
hardly to have changed in the course of the centuries. Once
again, one feels that time stopped at the Iron Age in the
mountains of the region; carts in use today differ very little
from prehistoric ones. Aside from the main highways, the
trails have not become more modernized in these thousands
of years, and they could not have been worse in the Iron
Age than they were till thirty years ago.

It was in the seventh century (phase *B* of the fourth
period) that the Camunians ventured onto horseback for the
first time; but there is some reason to suppose that riding was
a rather unusual activity. They seem not to have developed
much taste for this means of travel, for although mounted
figures do increase somewhat in number during the following
centuries, they never become really frequent. The horse apparently remained a luxury animal reserved for leaders or war
heroes. At any rate, those are the only figures shown mounted.
The other carvings in which the horse appears show it partici-

Four-wheeled wagon followed by praying
procession. Middle period IV, Naquane.

pating in funeral rites, in processions, in religious ceremonies.
The horse is still a special animal.

The use of oxen and horses as draft or saddle animals is
a custom foreign in origin, like the animals themselves. The
former appear in the chalcolithic period, and the latter in the
late Bronze Age. The wheeled vehicle, which was known
in Sumer since the beginning of the fourth millennium B.C.,
came to Europe only in the early part of the second millennium, by two routes: one through Anatolia and Greece; the
other through the steppes in the south of Russia, whence the
wagon reached the Balkans around the nineteenth century
B.C.[8] A small cart of terra cotta found in Palaikastro, in Crete,[9]
is probably the most ancient evidence we have of its presence
in Europe.

The rich collection of archaeological remains found at

[8] M. Gimbutas: "The Prehistory of Eastern Europe," *Bulletin of the
American School of Prehistoric Research*, Part I (Cambridge; 1956), pp. 68,
78; and *Sovietzkaya Archaeologia*, Vol. VI, p. 79.

[9] A. Evans: loc. cit., IV, p. 808.

different sites in Europe—fragments of wheels, miniature models, designs on ceramic, rock carvings, and paintings—proves that towards the middle of the second millennium wheeled vehicles had already reached Italy, and central Europe.[1] In the late second millennium they occur in Scandinavia, but in Spain they probably arrive only at the end of the second or at the beginning of the first millennium. The appearance of wheeled vehicles in the Camonica Valley in the sixteenth century is a landmark in its history.[2]

[1] In the Balkans and in Hungary wheeled vehicles were probably already known early in the second millennium B.C.; cf. *American Journal of Archaeology* (1959), p. 53.

[2] The spread of the Bronze Age war chariot in Europe is discussed in more detail in the *Proceedings of the Prehistoric Society*, 1960.

Four-wheeled wagon from early period IV, Naquane.

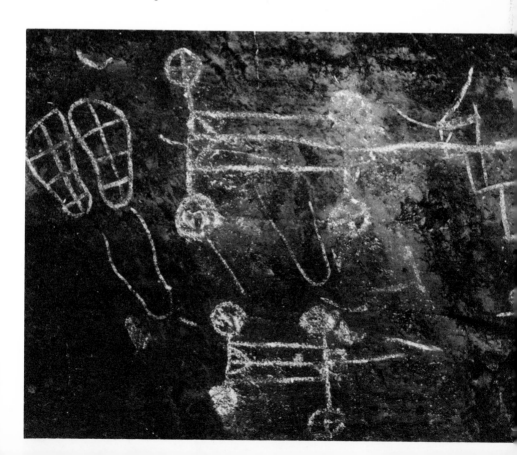

COMMERCE

In recent years great interest has been displayed in the commercial relations of prehistoric peoples of Europe, and innumerable theories on the subject have been proposed. In some cases the discovery of a few fragments of pottery, or of a weapon typical of a certain civilization, has been considered proof of contacts between widely separated peoples and of commercial exchanges whose importance is occasionally exaggerated.

We might perhaps better understand the nature of these contacts by observing first of all what occurs in our own times. Even today, certain villages situated off the highway are only visited by itinerant peddlers every two weeks or so. Traveling with their wagons over the poor trails of the region, these merchants bring the peasants tools, household utensils, fabrics, all kinds of products that the local craftsmen do not make. These are exchanged for cheeses or hides. This primitive commerce is centered within very narrow limits. Starting from the nearest large village, the traveling merchants rarely go beyond a radius of ten miles in their wanderings.

Business dealings, especially the sale and purchase of animals, take place once or twice a year at the fair held in the most important village of the canton, usually on the patron saint's feastday. This is the occasion for a great gathering of the inhabitants of all the surrounding villages. But the event is still local. Yet, the commercial exchanges that take place in the valley and the nearby mountains are probably more developed today than they were three thousand years ago. We would be mistaken, then, when we speak of contacts with the distant Mycenaeans or with Scandinavia, to believe that merchants from countries lying at opposite ends of the known world came to offer their wares in the Camonica Valley.

Amber and other merchandise from central and northern Europe arrived in Greece in the middle of the second millennium; Mycenaean daggers, helmets, and war chariots reached central Europe at the same time. The trading to which their presence testifies took place all along the international amber route. In the communities off this route, commerce was primarily a matter of successive hand-to-hand exchanges, thanks to which objects as well as ideas could travel to the periphery and little by little reach distant areas. The techniques of trade were rapid and simple only along the great transcontinental trail. This route crossed the Alps towards the Upper Adige, passing less than forty miles from Camunian territory. Camunian objects, especially weapons and the products of local metallurgy, would reach the great route; conversely, merchandise from foreign industry appeared in the Valley. This is doubtless the explanation for the presence in the heart of the Alps of Mycenaean war chariots, daggers, spears, and other items of foreign origin which the Camunian artists pictured on the rocks.

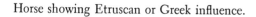

Horse showing Etruscan or Greek influence.

Commercial contacts within the neighborhood were more regular. They are already apparent in period II, in the lower part of the Valley, with the Remedello civilization; later they appear with the group of tribes in the center of Europe which make up the Aunjetitz civilization. In the late Bronze Age they become increasingly common with the farming villages of Terramare and of the Urnfields. It is at this point that the ring necklaces, the spiral "spectacle" pendants, and the new weapons originating mainly in those regions are gradually introduced into the Valley. These contacts continue through the first Iron Age, with the Hallstatt peoples for example, whose archaeological remains are often found not far from this region.

But it is not till the middle of the first millennium that we have evidence of the existence of more important foreign commerce affecting all of Camunian society. Clothing, helmets, shields, and offensive weapons in the carvings demonstrate that by then the products of Etruscan industry were widely distributed and integrated into the daily life of the Camunians.

7 · Religion and Beliefs

OF ALL THE problems raised by prehistoric civilizations, probably the most difficult to solve is that of religion. While it is sometimes possible through data provided by excavations to reconstruct a reasonable picture of the economic and social organization of the ancient peoples of that era, we are often reduced to erecting quite uncontrolled hypotheses where rites and beliefs are concerned.

As interesting and suggestive as are our findings in this realm in the Camonica Valley, we must nonetheless recognize that here, as in the other sites of central Europe, it is often extremely difficult to understand the significance of a vaguely discernible rite, to make out its main lines, and especially to learn in honor of what deity or spirit it was celebrated. Comparative material is needed to illuminate the problem; and unfortunately it is lacking. Our knowledge of the religion of prehistoric Europe is scanty: graves and cemeteries barely suffice to give us some idea of the cult of the dead; menhirs and cup-mark stones yield a mere glimpse of certain rituals. In this sense at least, although they do not entirely satisfy our curiosity, the carvings in the Valley present a considerable advantage over the discoveries heretofore made in this realm; scholars had not suspected the existence of so profuse an array of rites and beliefs as they suggest. They reveal extraordinary material, for instance, on the worship which the Camunians gave to the sun, to different animals (the stag in particular), to the dead, to heroes, to certain special places, to their temples, to weapons and countless other objects. They describe the Camunian pantheon, peopled by a horde of spirits and imaginary beings whose names remain mostly unknown; the faith in magic and sorcery; initiation rites, sacrifices, and the religious festivals the people celebrated.

Religion, then, must have played a very important part in the life of the Camunians. As was probably the case with most tribes of prehistoric Europe, the whole spiritual and intellectual energy of this civilization was centered on it and on the religious hierarchy of the tribe. Each person must have fulfilled a distinct and precise function. There are good reasons to believe that here, as in prehistoric Greece, "the house was a temple, the family a brotherhood, the father a priest."[1] And religion was a prominent element as well in the social and economic organization of the group.

[1] From C. Picard: *Les religions préhelléniques* (Paris, 1948).

Praying figure dressed in a short robe.

152

Scene with two people at the center who
seem to be quarreling. Behind each of
them, an animal. At the left, a building
within which two spectators are observing
the scene.

We know that this was true in a number of other regions
of Europe at the same period. In Gaul,[2] probably in Ireland
too, whole peoples were organized by orders, great families,
clans and tribes, which assembled then as they do today for
the annual festivals that recall archaic Celtic traditions. Caesar
and Lucian mentioned these gatherings among the Celts:
"Their religious festivals," they said, "were held in the woods
and outdoors rather than inside their temples." This is con-
firmed by the mass of religious carvings in the Camonica
Valley which are cut on rocks in the middle of the forest.

[2] Caesar writes: "Natio est omnis Gallorum admodum dedita religioni-
bus."

Detail of the great procession on the rock
at Naquane. The leader is dressed as both
warrior and priest, with lance and shield
and traditional headdress. Below, center, a
paddle. The leader is followed by a phallic
praying figure carrying an object (ax?).

To judge by the engravings, the Camunian feasts must
have consisted primarily of processions and sacred dances.
Similar dances and similar processions took place on various
occasions, at marriages and burials, as well as during all the

ceremonies celebrated in honor of the dead. It is interesting
to note that in the religions of the Cretans and of the Mycenaeans, about which there exists considerable iconographic
material, processions and dances also held a preponderant
place. The one represented on the walls of the palace of
Minos, in the so-called corridor of the procession, which depicted a ritual dance, is well known;[3] we also know the countless figures, paintings, and carvings on vases, jewels, and ornaments which show descriptions of ritual dances. The *Iliad*
gives us many descriptions of them as well.[4]

Present-day place names in the Camonica Valley per-
petuate the memory of a great number of open-air sanctuaries
dedicated to the gods. According to a local tradition, when
the Franks arrived, the village of Edolo (called Idul in ancient
times) still venerated the local deity whose name it bore and
whom Christianity had not managed to supplant. The village
of Borno, near which thermal springs flow, recalls the name of
the ancient Celtic deity Bormo, god of springs and healing,

[3] A. Evans: loc. cit., IV, p. 808.
[4] *Iliad*, XVIII, v. 590ff.

Praying figures in front of a bird.

whom the Roman writers had identified with Apollo. The Tonale Pass, the highest point in the Valley, retains in its name that of one of the most celebrated and most powerful divinities of Nordic prehistory; Tumer, or Thor, the thunder god.[5]

Birds seem to have played a prominent role in the Camunian religion, especially during the fourth period. The carvings contain a great many birds—on a temple, or beside a god, or between two warriors in mutual combat, as though to separate them or decide their fate. In other scenes a bird is pictured before a person who seems to be speaking to it. Thus it appears that the Camunians considered birds, if not divinities themselves, at least semidivine or associated with the gods. The same was often true in Greece and Rome. Nilsson has suggested that in pre-Hellenic Greece the bird might have been the symbol of divine apparitions.[6] Athena readily takes such form in the Odyssey.[7] Hera and Apollo often do the same. A great deal of archaeological iconography demonstrates that birds also played an important part in the religion of the Urnfield peoples. In Camunian art the bird seems to have functioned as protector of a person or a building: a warrior or a house.

At the center of the Camunian religion—whatever transformations it underwent over the centuries—lay sun worship and stag worship. The two constitute the theme of more than three quarters of the religious scenes in the Valley. It would be a mistake, however, to believe that these were separate cults; religion and mythology formed an indissoluble whole.

[5] It is very difficult to establish a date for the introduction of a northern divinity like Thor into the Valley area.

[6] M. Nilsson: *Minoan-Mycenaean Religion* (London: Oxford University Press, Inc.; 1927), I, p. 285ff.

[7] *Odyssey*, VII, 81. *Iliad*, 11, v. 547.

House with a sacrificial animal at left and
an altar at right.

Stone altar found near one of the engraved
rocks.

It is likely that the discoveries in the Camonica Valley will also provide us with information on the beliefs of other tribes and other peoples of central Europe, particularly the Celts, since at one point in their history the Camunian people shared in that Celtic culture. From Scandinavia, from Ireland, from Britain and Spain to the Upper Adige, the Celtic peoples and those related to them had a great many common traits among them. Nevertheless, each community, each group, developed on its own with a certain autonomy. The variations among them are many, and it is dangerous to try to construe a single culture from the whole broad sphere. But knowledge of the Camunian religion can certainly afford us interesting points of comparison and disclose, beyond the differences, a kind of ideological unity.

SUN WORSHIP

"The day came when man subdued the beast. The domestication of animals stunted the vitality of the totemic cults, which survived only insofar as they adapted to new concepts. From that moment on, man was dedicated to farming; he would look for the elements of his subsistence no longer exclusively in the uncertain yield of the hunt but in annual harvests as well. His gaze would turn with greater attention to the star of light and heat whose rays fertilized or withered the seed in the earth, bringing abundance or famine to the home or the stable. Each morning, these first farmers greeted the return of the fiery disc at the threshold of its celestial route; and, slowly the heliolatric religion grew."[8] Thus, half a century ago, Déchelette interpreted the relation between the

[8] See Déchelette in *Revue archéologique* (Paris, 1909).

Three houses, superimposed on earlier animals.

birth of the sun cult and the advent of agriculture. His explanation, however, does not always correspond to reality, and there is room for more detailed discussion.

The slow, irregular evolution of the first societies of Europe was seldom accomplished by abrupt changes; agriculture did not suddenly replace hunting and gathering. We know, for instance, that in the Camonica Valley hunting con-

159

tinued to be an essential element in the economy of the area until Roman times and even to the present day. In the Valley the sun cult often mingled with other kinds of worship, giving rise to strange and complex religious conceptions, which developed and took on different forms. The sun was part of the whole constellation of Camunian religious concepts and was linked to the fertility cult as well as to the cults of the dead, of ancestors, and of animals.

There is evidence of a solar religion in a great many prehistoric civilizations of Europe; rock art attests to its existence everywhere to some extent, but particularly in Scandinavia, at

Composition on the upper part of the great rock at Zurla. Lower left, a god pushing a solar disc toward a great stag surrounded by animals. Above, a labyrinth and footprints.

Mount Bego, and in Andalusía. Varying according to the region, it adapted to each, conforming to the way of life of the people and to their economic and social systems. In Scandinavia it is not unusual to see solar discs together with ritual boats bearing them;[9] often, too, the sun is associated with spirits or infernal deities. One curious conjunction is that of sun and stag; it is also very frequent in Camunian carvings.

At Mount Bego the sun disc is represented sometimes with oxen, around which the local worship is centered, and sometimes with weapons, especially daggers. One extremely interesting scene, reported on by Georges de Manteyer, shows the sun in its four phases: "the sun *underground*, the sun escaping from the earth, the sun beginning to throw its rays, the sun in full glow at the zenith.[1] This and other scenes like it are good examples of the conception of the sun which the inhabitants of Mount Bego had developed: to them, the flaming star that emerges from the earth each morning had spent the night in the world of spirits and the dead. The mythologies of ancient oriental peoples present singularly similar ideas.[2]

In the Sierra Morena, in the Laguna de la Janda, and in other parts of Andalusía, the solar disc is frequently associated with representations of the sexual act;[3] in that context it is the symbol of the fertility ritual which held a very important place in the religion of the peoples to whom we owe the schematic rock paintings of the region. From these examples we

[9] Brønsted: *Bronzealderens Soldyrkelse* (Copenhagen, 1938).

[1] G. de Manteyer: "Les dieux des Alpes de Ligurie," *Bulletin de la Société d'études des Hautes-Alpes* (1945).

[2] J. A. Wilson, in H. Frankfort and others: *Before Philosophy* (Maryland: Penguin Books, Inc.; 1951), p. 62ff.

[3] H. Breuil, M. C. Burkitt, and M. F. Montagu-Pollock: *Rock Paintings of Southern Andalusia* (London: Oxford University Press, Inc.; 1929).

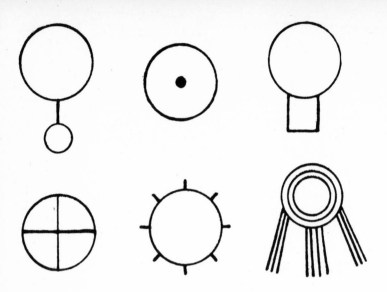

Various types of solar discs from style III
figures.

realise that sun worship occurred in Neolithic times and
in the Metal Ages among populations for whom agriculture
was not the principal means of subsistence.

In the Camonica Valley there are more than a hundred
scenes depicting sun worship; they are all extremely rich in
detail. The sun figures in them in different forms, all deriva-
tions of the circle. Shown above are the six primary ones,
which are repeated with many variations.

The most ancient Valley carvings dealing with sun
worship belong to the end of the Stone Age, to the second
half of the third millennium B.C. At that period the sun is
drawn as an isolated disc; seldom is it accompanied by a person with hands upraised in an attitude of prayer, or by an
abstract sign. Not until period II do true cult scenes appear
in which the sun is surrounded by several worshippers. Some
of these carvings show near the sun a figure very different
from the other people, schematically drawn and sometimes
without legs. We will discuss this figure further.

Period II also contains paired suns, one with its rays beaming outward; the other, inward. The latter, with a varying number of rays, is often given the aspect of a wheel. These pairs of suns with external and internal rays continue to appear frequently in the following centuries. A number of hypotheses have been advanced in an attempt to explain them, but none is truly satisfactory.

Also very frequent are scenes showing stags or other animals running toward the sun. The treatment of these is often quite simple: the artist contents himself with showing the two subjects side by side. But the variants are numerous: for example, the stags, instead of running toward the sun, may penetrate its circle. The sun then seems to have a kind of handle. Solar symbols of this type, in ceramic or in bronze, have occasionally been found in various sites; they were probably worn at the neck as a kind of amulet or good-luck pendant.[4] The meaning of this latter type of carving would remain obscure except that fortunately we have other, similar ones more naturalistic in style. One such engraving, discovered in the region of Zurla, shows a solar disc being pushed by a person wearing stag's horns—he probably represents the stag god. Under the sun, the artist has carved a stag whose head bears enormous antlers, and around him smaller animals appear. Should the interpretation be that the sun has the power to multiply the game? The cults of the sun and of

[4] It is of particular interest to note the resemblance in concept of solar standards, containing figures of stags or deer within them, discovered in pre-Hittite Anatolia. Cf. Remzi Oguz Arik, "Alaca Höyük: une nouvelle station proto-historique en Anatolie Centrale," *IPEK*, Vol. XIV (1940), pp. 23-35.

Animal entering solar standard.

Phallic figure masked or with core, with solar disc attached to penis.

fertility often merge, quite obviously. Another scene of the same kind shows an ithyphallic figure whose face seems to be masked; he wears a solar disc attached to his sex.

It is rather difficult to determine the relationship between the sun and the stag. Aside from the various carvings we have described, this relationship is also apparent in a figuration at Paspardo in which a solar symbol with rays takes the form of a stag's antlers.[5] Perhaps through simple graphic association, the prehistoric craftsmen assimilated the ramifications of the stag's antlers with the sun's beams.

In the fourth period the sun often appears between two warriors battling each other; it may be replaced, as in one case

[5] Cf. E. Anati: in *Bollettino di Paletnologia Italiana* (1957).

The "rock of sun worship" at Campanine. Cup marks, cup and ring symbols, solar wheels, and two huts, the lower of which has a solar wheel on top and a smaller one in the upper floor.

164

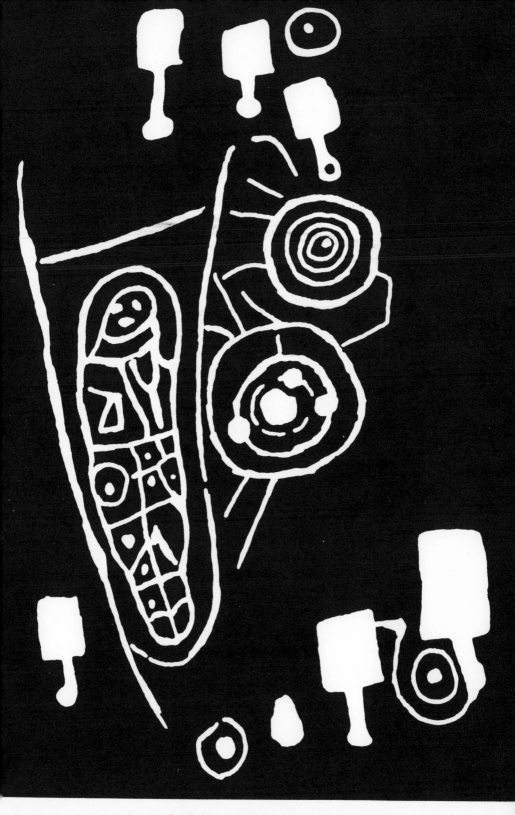

Symbolic grouping of an idol, solar discs,
and paddles, from Sonico. Style II.

we know, by a divinity, or by a mythological person holding a disc in his hand. This sun or sun person seems to have been considered a kind of judge or arbiter in combats, but the reason for the belief is not clear.

Finally, there are a great many representations of houses ornamented by a sun. They are probably temples of a sort. One rather complicated carving shows a construction decorated by a sun at the second-floor level, with a larger sun on the roof. The first story contains the altar and an ill-defined object which might be an offering. Outside is a kind of anthropomorphic symbol, a spirit or fantastic being without a body, its face shaped like a disc with eyes and a mouth. The cup-marked rock on which this curious engraving appears bears other analogous figurations; for instance, suns like those already described—one with its rays beaming outward and the other inward. The whole composition remains enigmatic. The most we can say is that these constructions were probably devoted to the cult of the sun and that its worship seems to have been accompanied by offerings and sacrifices.

The sun is still the principal subject of the monumental compositions in period III; an important group of carvings is devoted to it, but this time the pictures accompanying the sun figure are solely symbolic attributes or decorations. The study of the rocks at Caven and at Borno, the two rocks of Paspardo, and probably the second rock at Cemmo too, attests to this. These rocks, on which idols are probably depicted and which served as centers for worship, suggest that the sun god often wore the torque necklace and the spiral "spectacle" pendants as ornaments. The lateral discs might be earrings. Less frequently, these figures occur accompanied by daggers or by animals like stags.

This brief summary of the main groups in which the sun is represented traces the evolution of its cult through the

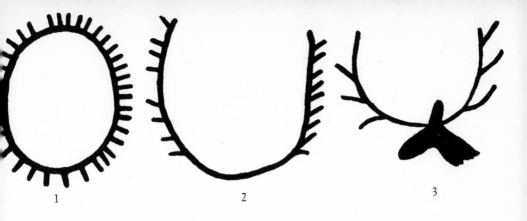

1   2   3

The horns of a stag or the rays of the sun?
In some cases it is difficult to know which
of the two the Camunian artist intended
to depict. (1 and 3) Cemmo; (2) Paspardo.

different stages of the Camunian civilization. Limited to
simple scenes of adoration in the Neolithic and Chalcolithic
periods and at the beginning of the Bronze Age, the sun later
becomes intertwined with many other beliefs and faiths,
notably those of the stag and of fertility. It then becomes a
deity decorated with ornaments and attributes, with its own
particular shrines. But apparently not till the fourth period, in
the Iron Age, did its ritual come to be celebrated within
temples or on esplanades. At that time it is surrounded by a

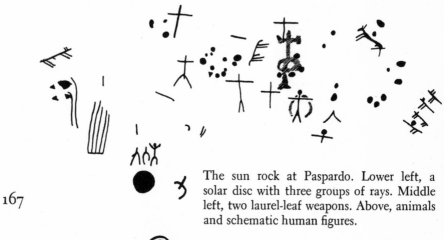

The sun rock at Paspardo. Lower left, a
solar disc with three groups of rays. Middle
left, two laurel-leaf weapons. Above, animals
and schematic human figures.

populous court of imaginary characters: spirits and mythological beings with supernatural and magic powers. At the very center of Camunian religion from its beginnings till the end of the third period, judging from the great quantity of carvings concerned with it, the sun later shrinks to the rank of one deity among many. New beliefs take shape in the fourth period, and the carvings dealing with these finally become more numerous than those of the sun. In the Camonica Valley the sun cult is mainly a Neolithic, Chalcolithic, and Bronze Age cult.

THE ANIMAL CULT

Animals were already the object of worship some twenty thousand years ago among the inhabitants of the Dordogne region, the Pyrenees, and the north of Spain, as their grotto-sanctuary paintings testify. The cult appears to have gained wide diffusion and a high degree of development from that time on. Through the centuries it can be traced in later epochs, under forms occasionally less highly evolved but always quite recognizable, in numerous parts of the continent, and in particular at Mount Bego and in Scandinavia.

The cult of animals left a deep imprint on the art of the Camonica Valley. There it was initially devoted to two animal deities: the stag god and the bull god. The worship of the stag god, which developed in the course of the Iron Age, seems to have been at the center of the Camunian religion in that period. The bull-god cult, which goes back to the beginnings of the civilization of the Valley, had only secondary importance by comparison. Apart from a few carvings dating from late in the third period, almost all the images of the stag god which we have found belong to period IV; thus the stag-god religion reached its highest development during the first millennium B.C. These carvings portray the god at the center of a circle of praying or dancing human figures. First represented as a stag whose forehead is crowned by enormous, many-branched antlers, it later takes on certain human attributes. Half-man, half-beast, it comes to be shown generally as a stag whose body is partly human. But after the fifth century B.C. it grows an entirely human body and the only vestige of its original form is its abundant horn structure. In an engraving at Zurla, the god seems to hold a bird in its right hand, and a serpent coils about its body.

The stag god (Cernunnos) was venerated during the second half of the first millennium throughout the whole zone of Celtic influence. Many evidences of this have been found. On

Deer cult in the transition phase III-IV, with a god who is half man, half stag.

a caldron uncovered at Gundestrup, a drawing shows the stag god in company with a serpent, as in the scene at Zurla.[6] The ritual consisted of prayers and dances performed around the god and of processions which probably took place in the course of particular ceremonies. Several carvings demonstrate that the rites were celebrated in places especially consecrated to this purpose—sanctuaries or temple esplanades.

At first glance, it might seem contradictory that the prime deity of the Camunian religion in the Iron Age should be fused with the mountain stag, the favorite game of the Valley hunters. But this is not unique; quite frequently primitive peoples worshipped the very animals whom necessity forced them to pursue and kill. To give an example, Father Francois-Xavier de Charlevoix relates[7] that the Canadian Eskimos customarily prayed to the animals they were setting out to hunt. We detect the same ambivalent behavior among the Camunians of prehistoric times. A scene from the great Naquane rock shows a group of armed figures performing a dance around a large stag which is standing before the temple, while a spirit[8] in the sky kills the animal. This ritual is analogous to the one Father Charlevoix reports. But to the Camunians, it was the celestial spirits who killed the stags; the human hand was only their agent. This concept is rather complex; we can but catch a glimpse of its broad outlines.

Still in the realm of hunting, we should mention the propitiatory rites practiced by the hunters of the Valley. They are only indirectly related to the adoration of the stag god. Numerous carvings show groups of people in prayer around an animal caught in a trap, or else praying before a dog that

[6] See Ole Klindt-Jensen in *Acta Archaeologica*, Vol. XX (1949).

[7] R. P. François-Xavier de Charlevoix: *Journal d'un voyage dans l'Amérique septentrionale* Vol. III (Paris, 1744), p. 115.

[8] *See* section on spirits and mythology, page 000.

Deer cult in middle period IV, with a god
who is still half man, half stag.

is chasing a stag. In some symbolic compositions the different
subjects are isolated, and one finds the signs of a worshipper,
an ax, and a stag side by side.

The cult of the deified stag, like that of Cernunnos in the
Celtic communities, represents the thinking of a hunting
people;[9] the bull and the ox, which were also worshipped by
the Camunians, seem to evidence the thinking of agriculturists. The carvings represent oxen, either free or harnessed
to the plow, in realistic style or schematically as horn-shaped

[9] At least in its initial stage.

171

Person with a weapon or tool. At right, an
ibex, perhaps under a spell.

A stag god fully human in form except for the antlers. The deity is festooned with a serpent. At right, small praying figure. Late period IV.

Horned god or mythological figure from Naquane.

or horned bovine heads. Pre-eminently an agrarian deity, the ox represented as a bucranium, an ox skull with horns attached, appears on the axle of a plow in a farm scene at Bedolina. The animals hitched to the plow are horses—or at least one of them is—which renders the symbolic significance of the bucranium design yet more obvious.

Worshipper in front of an ox. At right, a
weapon or tool.

The earliest manifestations we have found of the ox cult
in Camonica Valley come from the second half of the third
millennium—that is, still during period I. The cult grows to
great prominence during period II, persists through period III,
but disappears almost completely during period IV.

Inexplicably, the two major cults of the Camunians during the Bronze Age, the solar cult and the bovine cult, are apparently cults of agriculturists; yet hunting was by far the
most essential element of the Camunian economy. Conversely, in the Iron Age, when agriculture was as a general
rule better developed, the stag cult displaces those of the
sun and the ox, although it is usually associated with a hunting economy and way of life. This is quite surprising. Yet not
a single scene of an economic character indicates that agriculture might have retrogressed or become less important
among the Camunians during the Iron Age than during the
Bronze Age. In fact, the contrary should normally have been
true. Actually, despite incidental changes in the way of life,

173

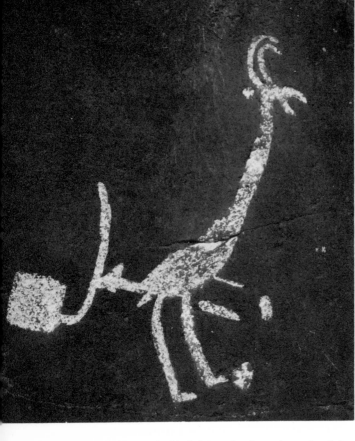

Fantastic bird from the Iron Age, dated by
the design of the ax near it.

Imaginary bird. Late period IV.

we have seen that hunting apparently remained the very foundation of the economic system of the Valley.

The religion of the Metal Ages in the Camonica Valley doubtless reflects the economy, but not necessarily the more general and permanent character of that economy. For reasons unclear to us, certain economic activities were able to inspire religion more than others. Tradition, too, may have played a paradoxical but fundamental role. The agricultural phenomenon—cultivation and the fertility of the earth as well as the relation between the growth cycle and the seasons —could have seemed most striking to this hunting people when they first discovered it. But once agricultural methods had grown familiar and become an integral part of the economy, the Camunians might have turned their interest to an earlier, favorite occupation.

Another possibility should be considered. For some reason, which we have so far been unable to detect, a shift might have taken place in the balance of the cults related to female and male occupations; as a consequence of this shift, more emphasis was given in later periods to rituals concerning hunting than to those related to agriculture. However, all these remain suppositions, and only continuing research can lead us to a solution of this riddle.

ALTARS AND SACRIFICES

The Latin authors left us remarkable documentation on sacrifice in the Celtic world;[1] it seems clear that human sacrifice was customary. Its purpose, we are told, was to appease Teutates-Mercury, Esus-Mars, Taranis-Jupiter, and a great

[1] Cicero: *Pro Fonteio*, X, II; Caesar: *De bello gallico*, VI, 16.

many other deities.[2] Tacitus reports that the Bretons washed their altars with the blood of prisoners and consulted the gods through the entrails of human victims. "This was in no way an act of reprisal or vengeance in their view but simply the execution of a religious rite."[3] Similar sacrifices were made to consecrate the foundation of a house or a public building. The Celts sacrificed animals as well; but this practice was also customary among the Romans, so the Latin authors did not consider it necessary to describe it in detail. Human sacrifices, however, seem to have made an enormous impression on them.

There is one carving in the Valley which may represent

[2] Cf. also: Dionysius of Halicarnassus: *Ant. Rom.*, I, 38; Justinian, XXVI, 2, etc.; Ann., XIV, 30.

[3] J. Vendryes: *La religion des Celtes* (Paris, 1948).

Funeral cart flanked by two funerary urns and followed by two horses with two altars. The armed figure at upper left does not seem to be a part of this scene.

Scene of human sacrifice? One of the figures appears to be fettered. Below, an ax of the Iron Age.

a human sacrifice—although this is not certain. A person who is apparently attached to or enclosed in a sack or a cloth is in the grip of a second, ithyphallic, figure who seems to be aiming a sword at him. At the executioner's feet is an ax. We have no other document suggesting the possible practice of human sacrifice among the Camunians.

The portrayals of animal sacrifice, however, are numerous. The scene with the executioner, his weapon, the sacrificial animal, and the altar, as isolated elements, is very frequent and characteristic. An ax and a halberd or a *cateia* are often carved over the head of the man. In other examples, the artist shows nothing but the sacrificial animal and the im-

177

1   2   3

Various carvings having to do with animal sacrifice. Figures (2) and (3) show two weapons above each person performing the sacrifice: an ax and probably a halberd.

molating dagger above him. We know only one instance in which the animal is pictured on the altar.

In one picture comparable to those already described containing the sacrificer, the altar, and the victim, an armless being who may be a spirit seems to emerge from the altar and move toward the executioner.[4] From this carving and others like it, we can deduce that the Camunians believed that a spirit or a magic force inhabited the altar. At the moment of the sacrifice, this force or spirit emerged and revealed itself to the sacrificer.

Neither the ritual dances nor the sacrifices apparently took place inside the temples or sanctuaries, but on their esplanades. The carvings often picture a sacrificed animal and an altar *in front* of a temple.

[4] On the spirit portraits, see section on spirits and mythology, page 00.

Funeral scene. Group of worshippers surrounding a corpse shown with his weapons and tools. At right, a person and an animal at an altar.

Funeral rite. Seven praying figures are lined up in front of the corpse. Beside it, an ax and other unidentifiable objects. At the right, a little temple with a sun symbol on the roof.

Scene of stag worship. Compare with page 29.

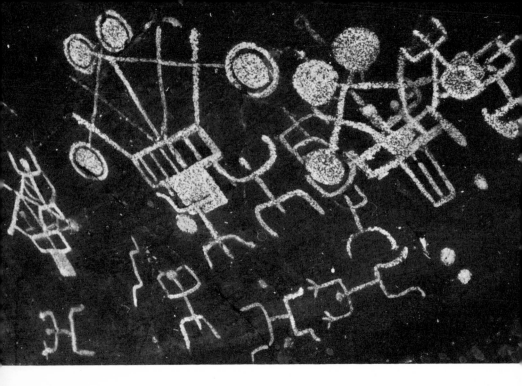

Worship of the dead, style III, overlaid
by two buildings of style IV.

The altars were of two principal kinds: the first, shaped
in the carvings like a chalice and executed entirely by stippling, was probably of stone; the other looks like a platform
raised on several feet and seems to be made of wood. The
repetition of the hatchet and the halberd in the sacrifice
scenes indicates that these two weapons were the ones ordinarily used. But the sword and the dagger also served at times.

Occasions for the offering of sacrifice must have been
frequent; yet the only scene that specifically indicates its use
is related to a burial or a funeral ritual. The sacrifice is performed in honor of the dead man, who appears in the center
of the carving and around whom a great number of people
are gathered in an attitude of prayer.

THE WORSHIP OF THE DEAD

To judge by the number of such scenes, the worship of the dead occupied the third place in the Camunian religion, after those of the sun and of animals. Through the centuries it took two different forms, one during period III exclusively, the other mainly during the fourth. The scenes belonging to period III show the dead person laid out on the ground; his weapons are arranged around him and prayers or dances are being performed before the body. A relative, or perhaps a priest, can be seen near the cadaver; he seems to be administering some last rites to the corpse. In the background, upright before the altar, a figure proceeds with the sacrifice; in one case we see also the animal he will immolate. In another scene of the same kind the animal is absent, but the setting is identical: behind the group is a glimpse of the façade of a small temple with a solar symbol on its roof.

In later scenes four-wheeled wagons occupy a prominent place. The funeral scenes of the fourth period show wagons carrying the urns in which the remains or the ashes of the dead are probably enclosed. A procession of worshippers follows the wagon. We have already said, in speaking of wheeled vehicles, that they were known from the beginning of the third period of Camunian art; but it is impossible to determine their place in the cult before the fourth period. Only on the large four-wheeled vehicles of the Iron Age do we see funerary urns.

The use of funeral carts was widespread in Europe during the first millennium B.C. One of them appears on a menhir

Mythological persons dancing or running. Note the bound legs of the horses. Late composition probably influenced by Etruscan elements.

statue discovered at Lagundo, in the Upper Adige;[5] others, on funeral slabs of the early first millennium from Estremadura. Still others decorate pottery fragments dating from about the same time exhumed at Ödenburg and in various sites of Germany, Poland, and Hungary.[6] At Ödenburg two men, one of them on horseback, make up its cortège. Remains of four-wheeled vehicles have been recovered in different archaeological sites of central Europe; in some cases they had been interred with the chieftains of the Hallstatt era.[7]

WAR AND HERO WORSHIP

It is only toward the end of the Bronze Age, around the year 1000 B.C., that the first battle scenes appear. This subject had never interested the Camunian artists until then; but henceforth it becomes very important—helmeted warriors bearing shields, spears, or lances occur with increasing frequency. From the 800's on we begin to see battle scenes showing two warriors in combat. They sometimes wear surprising plumed decorations and strange helmets. To the peculiarity of this array the warriors of Seradina, Bedolina, Zurla, and Nadro add another—their manner of battle resembles the steps of a dance.

Occasionally between the two adversaries or above them

[5] It has been argued that the picture of the wagon was added to this menhir statue several centuries after the statue was erected. The date of the statue itself is, however, very much disputed and at present little can be said on the date of the figure of the cart.

[6] W. La Baume: "Bildliche Darstellungen auf Ostgermanischen Tongefässen der Frühen Eisenzeit," IPEK (1928), pp. 25-56. Cf. also Joseph Déchelette: Manuel d'Archéologie Préhistorique Celtique et Gallo-Romane, Vol. II, p. 599.

[7] V. Gordon Childe: Prehistoric Migrations in Europe.

Gladiators in combat. Late period III or transition phase between periods III and IV.

Ithyphallic warriors. Iron Age, period IVB.

Warriors wearing strange garments. Period IVE.

Battle between two warriors in plumed
dress. Between them, a mythological being
holding a solar disc.

there appear spirits, imaginary beings or deities who frequently carry a solar disc in hand. Sometimes the disc is drawn
between the combatants; sometimes it is replaced by a bird.
As we have pointed out, birds were a manifestation of divinity among the Camunians. This curious symbolism leads us

Warrior of phase IVD, with antenna
sword and small round shield.

to conclude that such scenes represent more than simple armed
encounters. In our opinion these are gladiatorial matches
rather than battles properly speaking, and they are certainly,
in any case, celebrations of a religious rite. The presence of a
dead body in one of the carvings in this series suggests that
the dance–battle performed by the two warriors before him is

Gladiators. Transition period III-IV or period IVA.

in his honor. This does not mean, however, that in all cases the rite was related to the funerary cult.

The same ritual was performed among the Etruscans; a number of painted vessels found in the tombs, in fact, represent gladiatorial combats which took place during funeral ceremonies. Doubtless of Alpine origin, these games probably arrived in central Italy in about the sixth century B.C., at the time of the greatest Etruscan expansion, during the same surge of influence that so strongly affected the Camonica Valley.

It was much later that Rome in turn had jousting matches. The first sign of these dates from 254 B.C.; they formed part of the funeral honors rendered Junius Brutus Para by his sons, on the Boarium forum. They later became one of the most popular spectacles of Italy, but by then they had lost all their religious character.

In the Camonica Valley the combat of gladiators appeared towards the tenth century B.C. and took root very quickly. That the combats were religious in character is incontestable; they were performed not only on burial occasions but in other circumstances as well; for example, during

Small temple on elevated base, adorned with solar disc.

B

75

74

72

73

4

Southeast end of the rock at Nadro, showing weapons of period IIIB underlying
gladiators of early period IV.

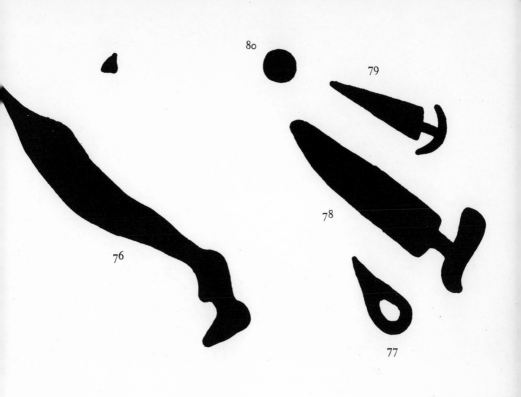

80

79

78

76

77

Figure with a short skirt, armed with dagger and shield and mounted on a running horse.

certain feasts honoring gods. The large-handed persons who also figure occasionally in the jousting scenes seem to connect them with ancestor worship.[8] In any case, from the eighth century on this was one of the most typical of the Camunian religious rites.

The same period of Camunian art brings to birth a new character, robust in body, his muscles bulging, bearing heavy weapons of exaggerated size. He is sometimes depicted standing upright on a galloping horse, or else battling imaginary

[8] See section on spirits and mythology, page 210.

190

animals, devils, wicked spirits, or other supernatural powers. This warrior god symbolizes the ideal; he embodies all the qualities necessary to the fighter: valor, courage, physical strength, and powerful weapons.

The hero occupied an important position among the Celts; in Irish and Breton folklore we find survivals of his role in mythology and of the worship accorded him. Tacitus says that the Germans worshipped a heroic figure whom he identified with Hercules.[9] Yet it is noteworthy that the Val

[9] Cornelius Tacitus, *Germania*, III, 1ff.

The death of a gladiator. Late period IV.

Dance or ritual combat? Mature style IV, showing Etruscan influence.

Camonica carvings in which this supernatural hero appears do not seem to be ritual scenes, but simply descriptions; they show his courage, his strength, his noble deeds. It is not easy to determine with any certainty his place in the Valley's religion. There is even reason to doubt that he belonged to the race of the gods. My own tendency is to interpret this figure as a legendary person whose adventures were so pleasing and so familiar to the Camunians that they loved to transcribe them on stone. But where to draw the line between mythology and religion in the Camunian belief? The parallels and fusions are often so close and so profound that it is impossible to distinguish the original elements from one another.

THE CULT OF WEAPONS AND OF OTHER OBJECTS

The hero cult and the bloody rites that accompanied it threw Camunian thought and beliefs into turmoil at the dawn of the Iron Age. In the Bronze Age this cult was still unknown, and instead, the carvings of that period give abundant testimony of a reverence towards weapons and tools which lent strength and glory to men. The veneration that originally surrounded such implements then turned to heroes. This veritable psychological revolution occurred between the tenth and the eighth centuries. Previously, the implement itself embodied power and strength; man was only an instrument, a means employed by the gods to maneuver it. In the Iron Age man played a role equal to that of the deity, so the frontier between them is not distinct and we cannot always tell whether the heroes are gods or men. The implement was now a means in the hands of the man–god to use to master the world, and it is he who henceforth will wield the supernatural powers with which the weapon was once endowed.

194

Worshipper in front of a house (of worship?).

Mythological figure with tail and horns, armed with lance and quartered shield. Last phase of style IV.

Warrior, showing Etruscan influence (fifth
century B.C.). Late style IV.

Detail of warrior, showing Etruscan influence.

The spirit's house. Within the house, two
oculiform figures. Below, a worshipper. Another human figure is approaching the
house from left.

197

The arms cult appears at the same time as the Camunian civilization; very early the weapon is pictured along with praying figures. Its size often surpasses man's because the weapon, not he, holds the power. The ax, the dagger, and the halberd are represented in many cases with the solar discs. In period III the dagger is a constant attribute of the sun god. It is shown under the disc with various other attributes, like the spiral "spectacle" pendant symbolizing fecundity, and the torque necklace. In the Near East and in Cyprus during the Bronze Age phallic-like spiral "spectacle" pendants are frequently related to the fertility goddess.

Certain flat rocks in the Valley are entirely covered with weapons. On one of them, at Nadro, the solar disc is drawn as concentric circles in the midst of weapons. A superposition of designs on this rock ideally shows the evolution of the cult—a weapon dating from period III is covered by a fourth-period carving of two gladiators in combat.

Camunian religion in the Bronze Age involves other objects of veneration. The plow, the wagon, and various work instruments also figured in the center of a group of worshippers and were honored. The paddle cult, which we shall discuss at greater length, is a similar phenomenon. In all these cases worship is directed towards human inventions that facilitate labor and, like the plow, yield greater results.

THE TEMPLES

The religion of the Bronze Age, with the worship it accorded to nature, the sun, trees, springs, rocks, mountains, and the earth, was a religion of the open air; its rites were celebrated out of doors. It is only at the waning of that Age, with

Building surrounded by an oval line and by
unidentified figures.

the birth of new religious concepts, that pictures of religious
buildings appear for the first time. The idea of the temple
probably proceeds from the conception which man developed
of the divinity; imagining it to resemble himself, he felt it
necessary to build it a shelter just as he constructed one for
himself.

Differing from our churches, which are gathering places,
the temples of antiquity were often simply the gods' homes.
If the temples occasionally reached immense proportions, it
was because they were meant to reflect the greatness of the
divinity, rarely because they were destined to shelter a great
number of worshippers. In Greece certain temples of the
most modest dimensions, like that of Athena Nike, were no

199

more than an enclosure for the divine statue. Moreover, only the priests were permitted to enter there, and the sacrifices, as we know, were performed on an altar raised outside on the esplanade. The same was true in the Camonica Valley; the temples there were always small in size. Seldom did they surpass the dimensions of a family hut. The ceremonies of the cult of the dead, the sacred dances, the sacrifices, the gladiators' games—all took place on the esplanades.

Aside from temples proper, the Camunian carvings show the existence of similar constructions which had a different purpose. One very curious scene on the great Naquane rock depicts a small house and two strange figures, probably representing spirits. Between the pilings one of them is seen in a posture of prayer; the other is walking towards the house. This scene, difficult to interpret, would seem to indicate that certain huts were a kind of "house of the spirits and of the ancestors." Some of these sacred huts, decorated with solar symbols, were probably consecrated to the sun cult, while others harbored an animal cult. Frequently whole herds are pictured running towards the temple; sometimes the sacred dances are performed outside it around a stag. And finally other huts, as we have mentioned, were dedicated to the worship of the dead. It is unknown whether these sacred huts, perhaps sorts of *marai*, were used for several cults or whether each was devoted to a particular cult.

There are many representations of sacrifices performed before a temple; the temple is always pictured at the center of the scene. At one side is the altar, at the other the animal

Phallic figure with a paddle, in front of a horned animal.

200

destined for immolation. But the symbolic bringing together in the same scene of a small temple, a dagger, and an animal seems to have the same meaning.

To judge by the number of carvings, the sacred huts were quite numerous in the Valley during the Iron Age. Some were probably raised in the midst of other dwellings, but most were built in remote spots, suggesting sanctuaries or sites restricted to worship. In the wooded areas, graven stones suited the purpose. In any case, the study of a mass of highly realistic scenes, rich in detail, indicates that the artists who carved them probably had before their eyes the temples they pictured on stone. More extended excavations might yield some traces of these temples.

THE PADDLE'S MAGIC

Magic and religion were closely linked in the beliefs of the Camunians, and it is often very difficult to distinguish one from the other. The sun, dispenser of sexual fecundity and of the fertility of the earth, on whom good and bad harvests depended, was accorded a religious worship that included performance of rituals obviously magical in nature. Conversely, certain magical rituals were part of religious worship: the sacred dance performed around the divine stag, for instance, was supposed to bring good fortune to the hunt; the mortal combat of the gladiators, which had a propitiatory value, banished evil spirits and appeased ancestors.

Sometimes, however, the separation is more definite and the ritual recorded in the scene is purely magical. The example of the paddle is probably the most obvious. We have given the name of paddle to a sign which resembles that object: a square or rectangular surface with a kind of handle

201

Stag with paddle sign.

to it. The handle sometimes ends in a circle, often pierced with a hole. We have found several kinds of paddle; the shape of the handle and its length in relation to the size of the square vary. More complex models occur, in which the handle ends differently; or instead of one paddle we find two joined together. In certain cases, we can reconstruct the size of the paddle by contrast to that of the person holding it. Thus, in a carving where it appears in the hands of a man presenting it to a horned animal, it seems to be somewhere between thirty and thirty-five inches long. Even if these dimensions are not exaggerated, and they probably are, it was a maneuverable instrument. In other carvings it is no bigger than half the size of the man holding it; there it would measure between twenty-four and twenty-eight inches.

Symbolic composition showing a stag running towards a solar disc. Behind the stag, a hunter; in front of it, a spirit bust.

Wooden paddles of somewhat comparable shape and size have occasionally been uncovered in the Terramara of northern Italy; but we cannot be sure that those are the same objects.

Animals, paddles, and a human figure without arms.

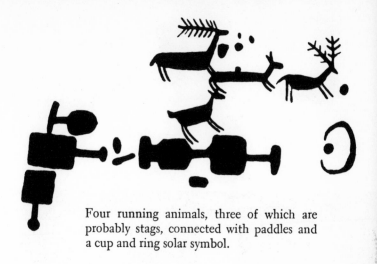

Four running animals, three of which are probably stags, connected with paddles and a cup and ring solar symbol.

The paddle was pictured with great frequency by the Camunian artists. On the great Naquane rock alone it appears sixty times, and at present some fourteen hundred examples of it have been found. Also, for a long time, well before I began my own investigations in the Valley, scholars had been struck by the constant repetition of this sign. It is the only one whose interpretation has given rise to dispute. Professor Marro and Dr. Fumagalli after long study concluded that in the last analysis it symbolized the Camunians themselves. Since they lived on the banks of a lake and a river which they navigated readily, this sign represented the oar of their boats,[1] according to these scholars. The theory, tempting as it is, has no foundation on evidence. No carving shows a paddle with either a boat or a fish, nor with anything related to water. But other researchers have gone even further; they contend that the drawing refers to "a paddle for beating laundry, like those still used today in different areas of central Europe." There have been several other interpretations as well. Some archaeologists have seen a razor in the design; others a double-edged ax.

[1] G. Marro: *Rivista di Antropologia*, Vol. XXI (1935); S. Fumagalli: *Atti della Società italiana di Scienze Naturali*, Vol. XCV (1956).

Stags running toward paddles.

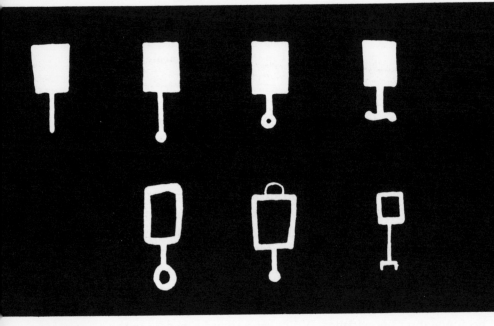

Types of paddles from the great rock at Naquane.

Two compositions containing paddle signs.

A sign resembling the Camunian paddle figures in various hieroglyphic writings—Egyptian and Hittite inscriptions among others. For the Egyptians it represented the tool of the architect. In the hieroglyphs its sense is *to build, to construct*. This is why, early in our labors, we sought the meaning of the mysterious symbol in that direction. But after close observation of the scenes in which it occurs, we decided that it could not have the same significance.

Comparisons with Celtic iconography turned out to be more suggestive. Among the Gauls, in fact, certain tribes venerated a being who held a mallet in his hand. Several authors have believed him to be a deity, without managing to identify him. God, spirit, or imaginary being, some twenty representatives of this figure are known. He is often pictured on altars, sometimes accompanied by a woman; this is the case at Sarrebourg, for example, where a dedication informs us that they are Sucellus and Nautosvelta. So far, the meaning of these two names remains a mystery. It has been proposed that Sucellus be translated as "good hitter," but this interpretation is not really convincing. On reliefs at Lyons and at Vienne, Sucellus carries his mallet in one hand and a vase in the other. Elsewhere, as for instance at Montceau (Saône-et-Loire), he is accompanied by a dog.

Whatever may be the identity of this Celto-Gallic figure, the tool with it greatly resembles the far more ancient paddle figurations in the Camonica Valley. It should be noted that in the Valley the paddle is seldom shown in the hands of a person; in the scenes and compositions where it appears,

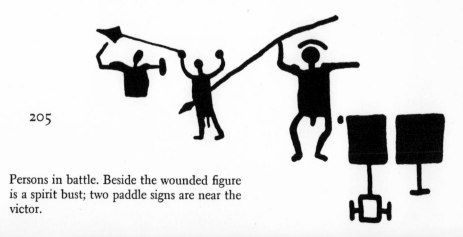

205

Persons in battle. Beside the wounded figure is a spirit bust; two paddle signs are near the victor.

Stag caught by a lasso, surrounded by paddle
signs. Middle period IV.

it seems always to have its own meaning. In the symbolic
carvings it is often placed in relation to a praying bust, which
represents, as we shall see, a beneficent and protective spirit;
or else with a stag or other wild animals, or with hunting
weapons. On one very curious carving it is held by an ithyphallic figure. The goat standing square on his four hooves before
the man seems fixed in position by a powerful spell. In another rather complex scene, very symbolic in character, the
paddle is associated with a solar disc; a person armed with a
lance pursues a stag which is running towards the sun as

though the paddle shown before him attracts him there. More frequent, but analogous, is a carving depicting a paddle along with an animal caught in a trap. Another curious hunting scene represents a stag entangled in a large net and a worshipper in contemplation before three objects: a stylized net, a paddle, and an instrument impossible to identify. On rock 50 at Naquane a magnificent stag caught in a lasso is surrounded by paddles. But it is a carving found at Zurla which first hinted at the solution to the problem. It represents a person armed with a lance, the animal he has just captured, and a paddle in which another animal seems confined. The most likely interpretation is that the animal caught by the man was trapped by the power of the paddle. This is doubtless the direction in which we should look for an interpretation of many similar scenes.

Battle scene in which a "small" man wounds a "big" man, the small man touching a paddle with his foot.

The paddle appears not only in magical hunting scenes; very often during periods II and III it occurs before a praying figure. At that time it must have been part of the cult of instruments and tools of which we have already spoken. During these periods it was sometimes associated with the sun and with the labyrinth. In one case, in the third period, it is represented on each side of a loom; elsewhere it appears near armed figures. Its role, then, must have been to afford protection. One carving from period IV, where it occurs instead of a shield, is somewhat comparable to other less explicit scenes in which the paddle accompanies the winner of a fight, the leader of a procession, the warrior on horseback in battle.

In war its protection insured victory, too. On the great rock at Naquane, where two horsemen are fighting two foot soldiers and one of the horsemen has just wounded an adversary, the conqueror is ringed by paddles; near the wounded man there appears a praying bust. The same symbolism can be checked in other scenes which set up a contrast between paddle and praying bust, victorious and conquered soldiers. And in one scene describing a ritual procession, a paddle is carved at the feet of the only figure mounted on horseback, who must be the chieftain.

A schematic oculiform representation of a human face.

From these examples we perceive to what concept this sign corresponded in Camunian thought. It is clear that it cannot stand for an oar or a laundry paddle or even a mallet, nor for any kind of utilitarian instrument; this is plain from any halfway conscientious analysis of the carvings. We may certainly suppose that originally the paddle had a practical character, and even that it was an object in common use. But

Mythological figure wearing a short skirt and surrounded by several objects, including an ax.

Figure without arms in front of a paddle, from middle period IV. Footprints and triangular dagger from late period IV.

as a symbol it was later applied to a score of situations. Hunting, war, religious ceremonies, daily labors—it is present everywhere; its original use was eventually forgotten, and only its magical attributes persisted. Thus, it is a talisman, a veritable good-luck image, a kind of sorcerer's wand. Its magical character is incontestable. It must have been extremely powerful, for all evidence indicates its immense popularity. The Camunians put great trust in it during the two thousand years of their existence.

SPIRITS AND THE CAMUNIAN MYTHOLOGY

Much has been written on the gods of the Celts, and the writers have not always restrained their imaginations. Almost everything we know about these people we owe to the Latin writers; but it is often difficult to know how much credence to give their testimony. The Celtic civilization they speak of, heavily impregnated already with Roman influences, was on the road to total disintegration at the beginning of the Empire, when they had occasion to observe it. Were the deities being worshipped at that late period the same as those of the early Celts? In addition, we usually know their names from translations into Latin, and since the Romans always exerted great effort to identify the gods of the barbaric peoples with their own, it is to be feared that their information may be somewhat distorted. As for the monuments of Celtic origin found in Gaul, like altars or divine statues sometimes containing dedications, they are rare and are themselves from a late period.

At the time of the Roman conquest, the Celtic gods whom the Latin authors call Mercury, Apollo, Mars, Jupiter,

Running figure wearing the traditional headdress of a priest, from Naquane.

Minerva, and so forth, were extremely numerous; very often they are found in pairs. These gods, and the veneration accorded them, varied from place to place, and from tribe to tribe. Those whom the inhabitants of the Camonica Valley worshipped sometimes lent their names to the localities where their sanctuaries stood. We have noted that the little village of Borno recalls the god Bormo or Borno; because he had the reputation of curing sickness and was the deity of hot springs, certain Latin texts identify him with Apollo. Edolo or Idul is also the name of a god, and so is Tonale.

Warrior with ritual headdress.

Stag man or stag god from Paspardo.

The "devil" scene: A mythological figure with beak and horns attacks two persons. At lower left, two other figures with right arms amputated.

If we wish to go further back in time, we must turn to the carvings, the only vestiges that may yield us information. Camunian gods were not very numerous. From the beginning of the art to the end of the Bronze Age, the main deity was the sun, which sometimes appears as a deity of fecundity. The stag god, then only a secondary deity, becomes the most important one in the Iron Age; it is doubtless the same god as the Cernunnos adored by the Celts in the late Iron Age. The hero–god of war finally emerges, and his importance increases from the sixth century onward. But around these deities there appear in the Iron Age a horde of supernatural beings, good and bad spirits or gods of second-rate importance. The numerous carvings showing fantastic beings with tails, horns, and beaks, or figures of diabolical appearance that combine man and beast, suggest the existence of a particularly exuberant infernal world.

The belief in a shadow world is common to many Iron Age tribes in Europe. According to Caesar, "the Gauls call themselves the issue of Dis Pater,"[2] the god of the earth and of the realm of hell. I have previously described the bull god who was very popular in the Bronze Age but whose cult declines nearly to the point of extinction at the beginning of the Iron Age. This progressive retreat coincides with the advent of the devil figure with bullhorns. The old god that is replaced by new ones is transformed into a chthonian deity and its power changes from good to evil. This metamorphosis of a god into a wicked spirit, occurring at the moment of a revolution in the religious concepts of a people, is not unique.

The Iron Age engendered whole regiments of fairies and spirits whose power, different from the gods', was exerted primarily in the small details of everyday life; new cycles of legends and myths were born along with them. Many magical

[2] Caesar: De bello gallico, VI, 18, I.

A herd of deer pursued by an ox-headed
god with a double lance, standing on a horse
hobbled as always when bearing a god. Two
dogs pursue the stags.

concepts expressed in these legends traveled through the centuries; some have persisted past antiquity and the Middle Ages
into our own days. All of European folklore was profoundly
influenced by them.

The new beliefs very soon put their mark on the rock art
of the time. In eastern Spain human and animal figures
yielded to schematic pictures of demons and spirits; in Scandinavia, too, a whole mysterious imaginary world grew up,
often close to that of folktales.

215

Margaret Murray, who was unaware of the transformation disclosed by rock art, stated in 1931 that the early people who inhabited northern Europe lived in the unforested parts, where there was good pasturage for their cattle, until the fierce tribes of the Iron Age moved in from the east "and to a great extent exterminated the people and the civilization of the Bronze Age. Those folk who lived in the wild parts escaped the general massacre and learned that their best defence was to strike terror into the hearts of their savage neighbors." This, she believes, may have been the origin of the stories of sorcerers and fairies living in the woods which have come down to us. Little by little the forest populations infiltrated the villages and mingled with the local populations, like the gypsies of the present day, but some of them remained in the forests and some were still living there in the Middle Ages, in isolated sections.[3] It should be noted that a total change in population did not always take place at the beginning of the Iron Age.

Labyrinth with oculiform face at center.

Instead, and more often, the transformations occurred in the realm of ideas and concepts. This would create an imbalance in beliefs between the villages and large centers and the isolated country areas which persisted in their old notions of nature and the powers directing it.

In the Camonica Valley there are a great many scenes

[3] Margaret Murray: *The God of the Witches* (London: Oxford University Press, Inc.; 1931).

Labyrinth with anthropomorphic figure at center.

showing the devils at work. On a rock near Scianica a horned demon with a beak in the guise of a mouth, armed with a fork, attacks two people who try to defend themselves. Other victims, stretched out at its feet, have lost their right arms. In the Naquane area a person is assailed by a very large demon with a face pointed like a beak. These battles between men and mythological or supernatural beings are frequent in the fourth period of Camunian art. Such scenes show how precise and definite the Camunian conception of these supernatural, fantastic creatures was and also to what extent medieval traditions were a continuation of Iron Age beliefs.

Beaked monster beating itself with two hammers.

In certain cases a demon is represented in abstract and stylized manner, as a labyrinth whose twistings end at the center of the image in two dots standing for eyes; a third dot sometimes marks the mouth or the nose. These are probably monsters comparable to those of ancient Greece: the legend of the Minotaur doubtless draws its origins from this kind of concept. Sometimes the monster is pictured within the labyrinth; sometimes he seems to be one with it, to be himself the

Magical dance around a symbol.

labyrinth. These figures are also very common in the rock carvings of southern Scandinavia, and they constitute one of the principal subjects of the Atlantic megalithic art which stretches from Galicia in Spain to Brittany and Ireland.

218

Mythological figure with tail and horns or long ears. Late style IV.

Imaginary figures of late period III.

Mythological being with long arms and a core. Middle period IV.

Often the figure looks like an ovary, with an opening and a twisting path that leads to the schematic monster face at the center. Curiously, in megalithic art this fecundity symbol seems to be associated with the cult of the dead. In the thought process of prehistoric peoples, as in modern psychology, it seems opposites often met. However, the conception of the labyrinth, as expressed in Camunian art and in the other rock art of Europe, remains rather obscure. The sign appears with fighting gladiators and with solar symbols, as well as in compositions dealing with the cult of weapons. The very rare naturalistic scenes tell us little more. But the battles and the monsters associated with the labyrinth probably have some connection with Cerberus and the other strange hybrid creatures who guard entrances in the mythology of peoples through the centuries. There is probably also a relation to the concept of the difficulties and trials which must be overcome to attain a new world or a new state of being. Death and life are associated; one must die to be reborn, whether it be by true death or by symbolic death in the initiation rites and other rituals of passage existing among primitive peoples.

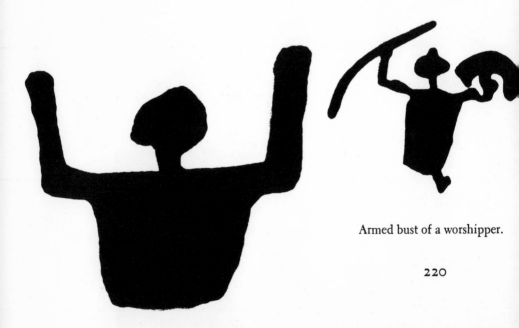

Armed bust of a worshipper.

220

Bust of a worshipper.

Types of busts from the great rock at Naquane.

Labyrinth with oculiform face at center.
Also a bird, a paddle, and a warrior.
Naquane rock.

Another very frequent figure in the Valley art is the one we have called the praying bust. It comprises the head and the upraised arms of a person in an attitude of prayer. This bust—the rest of the body is not shown—sometimes grips objects in its hands, most often weapons. The great Naquane rock contains thirty-four of them, and in the same region we have discovered more than four hundred. Some of these praying figures are linked with symbolic compositions; others oc-

Phallic figures with large hands in front of an armless and sexless anthropomorphic figure.

Phallic figure with large hands.

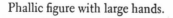

Types of human figures with large hands,
from the great rock at Naquane.

cur in hunting, war, or religious scenes. When they are part
of a scene, they are often placed above it, outside the action
as if they did not participate in it; they seem to observe or
to protect. They are also found near corpses. In war scenes
they appear beside the wounded. In the ceremonies of the
stag cult they are armed and kill the animal, while human
figures dance or pray around it. In the hunting scenes they
appear at the hunter's side; they follow the chief in religious
processions. It is very difficult to define more specifically the
role of this strange being or spirit.

As figures of the same kind we should mention first certain
creatures with large hands and second other beings completely lacking arms. The large-handed persons generally have
sexual organs of immense size, too. They are found in three

different types of scenes, often in groups of three or four, and they seem then to be praying or dancing. They are sometimes surrounded by wild animals, mostly stags, which seem to be running about them in all directions. They are also present at funeral ceremonies; in some instances they can be identified with the corpse itself, and in such cases it is the dead man who takes on the large hands. These strange beings, then, could be spirits or dead men. But, in that case, how can we interpret the fact that so many of them have outsized sexual organs?

Human figures without arms, from the great Naquane rock.

The people with large hands are rather common in a number of rock sites; their meaning is probably the same in all of them. Georges de Manteyer, who studied one such figure in the Mount Bego carvings in the French Maritime Alps, compared it to an Egyptian hieroglyphic sign which it resembles. This hieroglyphic is read as *cha-ka* and means "end" (*cha*) "darkness" (*ka*). Thus, according to Manteyer, the large-handed figure at Mount Bego would be "the spirit in every man . . . the irresistible power of virile force . . . the supernatural power which imbues magic, the sorcerer *hekacha*."[4]

[4] G. de Manteyer: "Les dieux des Alpes de Ligurie," loc. cit.

Labyrinth with geometric meanders similar to Greek coins. Late period IV.

Person praying before a headless being.

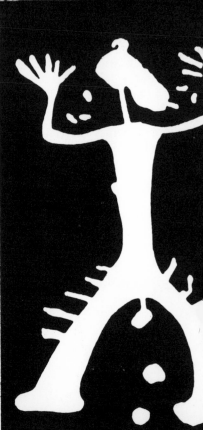

Large-handed figure with ornamented legs and strange headdress.

The large-handed figure in the Camonica Valley seems to be endowed with another power: that of casting a spell on game and drawing it to him. Where he is, the hunt is good; and inversely, where the hunting is good, it is because he is present. All this gives us a vague idea of a concept which apparently relates successful hunting to ancestral worship and of a whole association of complex and sophisticated beliefs and rituals. Confronted with these glints of Camunian mythology, we realize that we still know desperately little about the rich intellectual world of Iron Age peoples in central Europe.

We have mentioned in passing the carvings of figures without arms; they are found in the most surprising places, and at present we are not sure what meaning should be ascribed to them either. An armless being appears before two persons with large hands; another seems to emerge from an altar and direct itself towards the executioner who is about to perform a sacrifice. A third stands before an altar with an animal on it. Often they occur beside animals, especially stags; one of them appears above a house of worship. But the number of these carvings is still too small to permit a comparative analysis of the subject.

Hero on horseback, served by a man who leads his horse by the bridle.

227

Finally, we should mention a great number of isolated figures that probably represent imaginary and mythological beings, spirits, or forces of nature whose exact interpretation escapes us. Carvings have also been found of human faces in a schematic design somewhat comparable to those on megalithic tombs and on some statue menhirs. There are, in addition, headless beings before persons in prayer and schematic human figures in the shape of a *phi* Φ , probably linked to the solar cult since they are often found near a sun.

Thus, the carvings of the Camonica Valley reveal an extremely rich religious, magical, and mythological world. It is still too soon to try to explain it in detail. For the moment we are bound to generalities. From what we can make of it, this world appears in any case to be at the source of mythological traditions that have been transmitted to us first orally and then in writing and also at the basis of the occult sciences, of magic and of the beliefs which virtually dominated thinking until the Middle Ages and continue even today to influence it. Now we can be sure that in central Europe the majority of these beliefs were born with the Iron Age, at the beginning of the first millennium before Christ.

Religious procession on the great Naquane rock.

Human figures with headdresses, from the great rock at Naquane.

THE EVOLUTION OF CAMUNIAN RELIGION

The rich brown earth of the Camonica Valley was turned by the plow and the pick; it was seeded and tended; and it yielded its fruits. The fields were rich, industry flourished, the villages prospered; pastures gave food to the herds and the woods teemed with big game that was trapped as quickly as snares could be set in the undergrowth, in the grass and low limbs. Man was in constant contact with nature, and he felt its mystery; he sensed forces there that were greater than he. So at the dawn of Camunian civilization he turned to them; he pledged his devotion to them, and his prayers. At the center of his religious beliefs he had put the sun; its morning arrival, its journey through the sky, and its sinking under the earth at night led him to imagine complex relations between that star and the dark world of the earth, the home of the dead and of ancestors.

He had also made divine the bull and the ox, which he had learned to domesticate, had harnessed to carts and plows, and whose subjugated power was ten times a man's; they were accorded preferred positions at the center of his pantheon. Similarly, he found divine powers in the weapons and tools that increased his own strength and the possibilities of his arm and hand; they were divine themselves or at least divine creations of supernatural power, and he adored them.

229

In this context, man never considered himself a creator, but only an implement, an object. His acts were only the expression of a will outside his own. This archaic conception of the universe, of the laws that rule it, and of life, was to change later. At the end of the Bronze Age, when Camunian civilization was already a thousand years old, its pantheon grew richer and at the same time took on a different character. The sun would sometimes appear as a human figure, a highly stylized one; the gods were to take on human form. At the start of the Iron Age the stag god appeared as the god of hunting in the woods and mountains; later, another deity appeared, the hero–god of war. The divine stag, originally animal, would soon grow human, too, and towards the fifth century retain nothing of its old appearance but the antlers on its head.

At the outset of the first millennium a whole multitude of demons and spirits was born, an entire hybrid world which was to survive by far the civilizations that had engendered it; this fantastic mythology was accompanied by an array of magic rites used to ward off the evil eye, to exorcise or conciliate the spirits and ancestral souls, and to insure rich harvests and good hunting. Alongside the basic religious dogmas, each belief grew multiple variations.

The veneration of rocks, and with it the custom of covering them with drawings, appeared in the late Stone Age. The first carvings in the Valley seem to have a religious significance. Originally they are symbols: solar discs, weapons, praying figures, paddles, labyrinths, and so on; then they grow more complex, during the second period of Camunian art. The archaic symbols yield gradually to more realistic and descriptive representation; action is implied, and a relation is established between the different subjects. Around the sun or an animal or a corpse, groups of praying figures form. There is an effort to catch the image of reality. At the end of the third period, besides religious and ritual scenes, there are scenes describing acts of sorcery, magical agrarian or hunting ceremonies. Soon the Camunian artist becomes interested in depicting what he sees and does, in setting forth his daily life and the framework around it. Reaping, hunting, the various occupations of the Valley's inhabitants take a preponderant place, to the detriment of religious scenes. The fourth period of Camunian art narrates in detail the work and days of the small population inhabiting the Valley; handicrafts, stock farming, animal bartering, even erotic scenes inspire a whole new iconography on the rocks. Is there a link between the symbols of archaic worship, now disappeared—between the religion of early times—and the late Camunian iconography?

A new spirit has superseded the old, a new dynamism pulses in man; henceforth he manifests a different attitude toward his fate, toward his life, toward nature. Here in the Valley it happened with the advent of the Iron Age. Man ceased, at that date, to be an object abandoned to the occult forces of sky and earth; he grew aware of his dignity, his strength, and his potential. Larger in his own eyes, he begins to conceive of the gods and of natural forces as shaped in his image. Then the grottoes, the woods, the springs and mountains—all of nature—become peopled with a horde of hybrid beings, good and evil, little rustic gods, family demons, imps—which religion assimilates and whose traces are discernible at the very foundations of modern beliefs.

8 · Camunian Society

SOCIAL ORGANIZATION

EVERY CULTURE gives evidence of the society that gave it birth. A tomb, a primitive dwelling, a drawing, a fragment of pottery, a flint tool—all reveal a way of life, a social organization with its laws, its hierarchy, the bonds that join the members of the community. Reconstructing society is one of the first aims of archaeology. Unfortunately we manage only rarely to discern very many traits of the society whose remains we have discovered and studied. But the facts are there. We must always keep in mind that all archaeological remains are the products of a certain economic, social, and technological way of life.

In the Camonica Valley documentation is immense. It is impossible to foresee all the details of social organization which will be revealed in the final analysis of the twenty thousand rock pictures. This study has just been started, but we shall present here some data that will give a general idea of the life of the Camunians.

As the reader may have noticed, the scenes of a religious nature contain the largest number of human figures. How far these images are a faithful representation of reality is uncertain: especially in the archaic phases, the prehistoric artist often used the simple plural to signify a crowd. But counting the persons shown in the different scenes is not as futile as might at first be supposed. Rock 50 at Naquane, for example, has thirty-eight praying figures; at Coren del Valento a scene of worship shows sixteen. The religious procession depicted on the great Naquane rock is comprised of thirteen persons. Funeral ceremonies generally assemble a smaller number of participants: twelve on the great Naquane rock, nine on rock 35, eleven on a rock at Campanine, and so on. To indicate war, the Camunian artist sets only a few warriors against each other, fewer than seventeen most of the time, except in a scene discovered in the Bedolina region which contains forty. To describe the economic life of the area, even fewer persons are required. Laborers form groups of three, four, or five, never more; hunters usually two, but often only one; herdsmen one or two. The craftsman is represented alone, but he is a specialist. If someone stands near him, it is generally a young apprentice. There is one exception, however, the only one so far discovered: it is the weaving scene, already described, in which seven persons are at work. But weaving was, as we have seen, a well-developed industry with the Camunians; in two instances we find two looms working at the same time. This is why, despite the great number of pictures of houses and the many village and field plans—which would seem to indicate an economy based on the family unit—there are strong reasons for believing that in some realms a kind of collective work organization also existed. For the construction of temples, for example, help must have been recruited from the whole tribe, or from an entire clan. As to the fields, we have already said that their accurate planning, their distribution, their canals and walls presume collective work systems. Conversely the maps of villages show houses with small annex buildings, probably family granaries and barns; but no carving known depicts what might be a public granary or storehouse.

The diagrams of fields include a space reserved for animals, a vast pasture where all the cattle were gathered. Does this mean that the herds were collective property? We recall that horses were ridden only by chiefs and warriors. We cannot say whether that animal, rare and precious in the Valley, belonged to the clan or to its chieftain. The ritual carriages used in religious ceremonies, usually followed by processions of worshippers and associated with the cult of the dead, were probably the property of the community or of its leader.

Each clan or each tribe had its special identification signs and property marks. Weapons and implements were private property, however. Somewhat in the manner of clothing, they were part of the very personality of the individual who used them. In the carvings they symbolize the occupation of the figure holding them. Weapons, for instance, by their shape and size, indicate the role of the warrior wielding them, and also his prowess in jousting or war. They are an extension of the body of their owner and as such follow him into the tomb after his death.

The Camunian economy, as we construe it, must have been based essentially on individual labor, but the materials of production—the earth, the animals, and certain means of transportation or of work like the wagon—seem to have been communal property. In all realms of the economy as well as in war and in jousting, the heroes, those who killed the biggest game or reaped the best harvest, must have earned a position of privilege in the community. They were admired and envied, and their feats were chiseled onto rock.

CHIEFTAINS AND PRIESTS

The chieftain appears very late in the rock pictures and is easily recognizable. He travels on horseback preceded by his servant or his slave, who holds the animal by the bridle. In the religious procession on the great Naquane rock everyone moves on foot except him. He bears arms of war and is dressed in the elaborate costume of a priest or sorcerer. Evidently he has the attributes of both privileged groups. Behind him walks a person carrying an ax.

We have already spoken of the figure with a headdress of plumes who in the carvings participates in religious ceremonies, performs a sacrifice before a temple, separates two battling men, serves as arbiter, or, as at Naquane, leads a procession. In the last instance there are two of these figures, the only two in the group who carry no weapons and do not have their arms raised in prayer. The plume decorations they wear apparently indicate their function.

At the time of the Roman conquest the druids held a well-defined position in Celtic society which Caesar described with great care. "They preside," he says, "at the public and private sacrifices, and they rule religious practices; the young people come to learn from them and they are greatly honored. It is in fact the druids who decide almost all conflicts between states or between individuals."[1] They were at once priests, judges, and educators. And as members of one of the highest classes in the society, they did not go to war and may even

[1] Caesar: De bello Gallico, VI, 13, 1, 5.

235

Armed warrior.

Figure on horseback, led by a servant.

have been exempted from paying taxes.[2] Diodorus, in his description, shows them to be wise men to whom particular reverence was accorded. "They read the auguries," he says, "and predicted the future through the immolation of victims; no sacrifice took place without them."[3] Dion Chrysostom says that their social and political power was considerable; he adds that they were "versed in divination and in every other science; without them the kings were not permitted to take action or make decisions, so that they were virtually in command. The kings were only servants and ministers of their will."[4] It

[2] Ibid., 14.
[3] Diodorus: v. 31, 4.
[4] Dion Chrysostom: *Orationes*, 49.

The "marriage" scene at Nadro. At top right, a couple surrounded by praying or dancing figures. Below the couple, a schematic ox skull.

is uncertain, of course, to what extent these descriptions are reliable.

The carvings in the Valley dealing with this subject are neither numerous nor varied enough to tell us whether the Camuniân druids, long before Caesar and Diodorus' time, possessed the powers that the ancient writers ascribed to their successors. All we can see is that they attended the sacrifices and did not go to war. The procession scene indicates in effect that they bore no arms; that is particularly explicit in the context. We also gather from examining this scene that those who participate in the procession are divided into two groups, one centered around the chief, the other accompanying the two druids.

The oldest drawings of druids found in the Camonica Valley date from period IV; they would seem, then, to be an institution born in the Iron Age. But it apparently developed very rapidly; beginning with phase C of the fourth period the druid figures are more and more frequent. This suggests that they had grown very important by that time and had profound influence. Most of the scenes in which they occur date

237

from phases *C* and *D*. Later their number grows markedly smaller—a phenomenon contemporary with the perceptible increase in carvings of warriors and heroes in phases *D* and *E*. This is perhaps more than coincidence.

THE INDIVIDUAL AND THE FAMILY IN CAMUNIAN SOCIETY

Specialization is a very old phenomenon in the Camonica Valley. Since the third period the weaving scenes attest to the system, and so do the scenes at the forge. It probably characterized as well other kinds of work not depicted in the carvings particularly mining, which requires experienced specialized labor. The monumental art itself testifies to the existence of bodies of specialized workers; the Valley carvers must have devoted considerable study to the religious iconography and the manufacture of idols. Beginning with period IV specialization increases. The druids appear; they must have been numerous at one point. At the same time the notion of the chief, indistinct earlier, can be seen developing. The carvings evidence the respect given him and the honors his position earned him.

With the sixth century, war also became the business of specialists. The armed men who invade the carvings at this time must have been—at least to some extent—professional soldiers. Fighting possible enemies was their responsibility, and their importance in Camunian iconography must correspond to reality. Later, in the fifth century, there occurs a kind of general mobilization: all the men bear arms. Only the blacksmiths and a few other craftsmen were exempt. A considerable decrease of the productive segment of the population

238

Types of huts. The one in the center seems to be under construction.

Small building.

must have resulted, accompanied by an increase in the demands made on these people. Caesar tells us that in his time the Gallic tribes had recourse to taxes to meet the expenses of the State.[5]

Women seem to have occupied a considerably lesser position. At most they appear working the fields with men, tending cattle, weaving at the loom. Certain dances and rituals, however, seem to have belonged to them alone. Weddings were an occasion for a ceremony in which the whole clan participated. A scene at Nadro depicts a couple and before them a group of persons dancing or praying; stretched at the feet of the newlyweds is an ox. It is difficult to determine whether the ox symbolizes the dowry of the couple or the presence of the bull god at the ceremony or whether it is simply the nuptial banquet. Children are rarely seen in these carvings. However, one amusing scene at Seradina shows a woman working in the fields with her child on her shoulders. In other drawings men and women hold children in their arms. One scene, whose meaning escapes us, shows an ithyphallic figure with an infant in his arms before a pair of copulating animals.[*]

The meager social importance accorded women is brought out clearly by the statistics we tabulated north of Naquane. On an average, six out of ten human figures are masculine and phallic, and four are of indeterminate gender. Definite representations of women are very rare, no more than four per cent. Aside from scenes of prayer or dancing, women are generally not to be found in the carvings. The noble offices, like hunting and war, were man's exclusively; to woman were delegated the perpetuation of the race, weaving, and probably tending the home. The women also participated with the men

[5] Caesar: *De bello gallico*, VI, 14.
[*] Cf. *Man*, No. 145 (London, 1960).

in working the farms, (see p. 117) but they did not drive plows, for this was a masculine function (see p. 115). Among the engravings that do show women, some picture the sexual act. Here we should mention in passing certain carvings representing the coupling of a man and an animal, particularly a donkey. Other erotic scenes record the whole gamut of the vices of the time.

The houses in the Valley were generally small. They were sometimes built on piles; but more often the ground floor was used as a barn or granary. An outside stairway led to the living story. Beyond this, they differed considerably from one another. The six hundred figures of houses which we have found vary in dimensions and architecture. Some are small and very simple in appearance; others are larger, apparently handsomer, and covered with ornamentation. The artists probably wished, rather naïvely, to bring out the different social and economic levels of their inhabitants.

In the topographic carvings of the third period the houses have a more homogeneous look; but the drawings aim at simplicity. Some of the buildings are flanked by a small barn, the only visible sign of wealth. In the fourth period the differences begin to grow more marked, probably paralleling the transformations taking place in Camunian society. The chieftain's house and those of people of special rank are easily distin-

A Camunian of the Iron Age, wearing a short kilt.

guished from the others. The architecture, then, reflects the hierarchy that had established itself among the members of the community.

THE CLAN AND THE VILLAGE

In the carvings the Camunian villages are drawn either in ground plan or from the front. The superpositions show that the ground plans are usually earlier than the others—they date from periods II and III. The front-face representations only appear at the end of the third period and through the fourth. Thus, the former go back to the Bronze Age and the latter to its last stages and to the Iron Age.

The style of the ground plans is rather realistic; the landscapes, the fields, the villages, and the houses were probably before the artist's eyes as he cut into the stone. Let us examine the boundary marker at Bedolina, for example. On it we see some fields devoted to agriculture, others to stockfarming; at the top is a twisting stream, and below a village with houses. But this section of the carving is more recent—it is drawn over other figures. If we look at the Valley around the rock, we see that the stream still flows where the prehistoric artist drew it and the division of the fields has scarcely changed in three thousand years.

These diagrammatic Bronze Age maps are quite numerous in the areas of Pozzi, Bedolina, and Seradina; they depict small villages or hamlets with houses of slightly varying dimensions. The aggregations of dwellings covered rectangular areas here and there amid the fields; originally they were not very extensive. A few houses had enclosing walls and gardens planted with trees. Some of them were isolated in the country

House with stairs.

side, but more usually they were grouped in threes, fours, or
fives. Occasionally a building was flanked by a smaller one,
probably a stable or granary. Sparsely populated though the
Camunian villages were, there seem to have been a great
many, at least to judge by the quantity of maps. During the
Iron Age the villages grew larger. Isolated dwellings and little
hamlets still occur, but in the Naquane area we find communities of fourteen, sixteen, and nineteen houses. One of
true village size, near Campanine, has twenty-three. The Iron
Age houses are varied in size and shape, but the schematic

character of the figures does not always allow us to form an exact idea of them. They are isolated in the carvings, as though set in a void. Perhaps the wavy lines that connect some of them should be interpreted as paths.

It is interesting to compare the picture given by the maps with the archaeological remains. In the regions containing carved rocks one often comes across the ruins of dry-stone walls, prehistoric enclosures, or boundary markings, and beside them an occasional small house or two. From what we can deduce, the foundation was stone and the superstructure wooden, which explains why they have disintegrated. But the ruins that can still be made out generally date from the last centuries before the Roman conquest. The earlier houses must have been constructed entirely of wood, for they have left no visible trace at the surface.

Vestiges of larger dwelling centers are rare. Two or three have been found in the Valley. These date from the Iron Age and are located on fortified hills, always in a key strategic position, called *castellieri* by Italian archaeologists. They were scattered throughout the whole region in the late Iron Age. These small "castles," sometimes no larger than modern houses, were probably used as living quarters for local chieftains.

Combining archaeology and the analysis of the carvings, we can put together a rather clear picture of the distribution of the Camunian population. It was generally concentrated in small groups of between one to five huts during the Bronze Age. In the Iron Age there is evidence of a few rare instances of greater aggregations. Even less frequently veritable villages grew up. In the late Iron Age, as the function of the chief increased in importance, he would build his fortified castle on the summit of a hill and survey his realm from there.

It is difficult to determine the size of the Camunian

Rock of saints. Prehistoric imprints of six
carved hands which local folklore considers
to be those of three patron saints of the
region. Slabs situated in the crypt of a
church.

population during the Metal Ages. The agglomerations being
very small, the carvings must give a rather accurate rendering
of reality when they show thirty-eight persons participating
in a religious ritual or about forty warriors in battle formation.
The adult male population of each group must rarely have
exceeded that number. If, as it seems, in the early Iron Age
the Valley consisted of some eighty to two hundred hamlets,
and if we assume an average of fifty people in each, the population of the Valley must have been somewhere between 4,000
and 6,000. In the Bronze Age the population was probably
even smaller.

245

The situation changed in the last phases of Camunian art. Some villages soon included twenty-three houses. At the same time, isolated dwellings appeared in the surrounding area, like the beginnings of suburbs. Slowly the primitive hamlets of the Valley turned into real villages. The houses, originally made of wood and perhaps of earth, began to be built of stone in phase D of period IV.

The distribution of the carvings along the Valley reveals a certain geographic concentration of subject matter. Around Boario, near a lake which at that time existed in the Valley, fishing scenes are more abundant. At Bedolina and at Seradina agricultural scenes are preponderant. And in the mountains on either side of the Valley, from Giadighe to Cimbergo, hunting scenes predominate. Handicrafts—forges and weaving workshops mainly—were concentrated around Naquane. The pictures of that area also contain the largest villages and the greatest number of them. Moreover, the largest quantity of carved rocks occurs around Naquane. But the unity of style of the carvings, their very conception, attests to a close contact between the different regions of the Valley. The villages were not far from each other, and relations must have been maintained easily. If each region had its own economic character, it was because commercial exchanges permitted such an arrangement. In addition to an economic organization and the cultural and religious concepts which united the Valley intellectually, we can assume that in the late Iron Age a single social and political system held the Valley's inhabitants together as well.

Religion had important centers where the entire population gathered at certain times. These great assemblies, comparable to the Breton *pardons* or to our pilgrimages, bound the villages and provinces still closer. And marriages, which occasioned the intermingling of groups, would also fortify and accentuate that unity, rendering it more concrete and profound.

The language, too, must have contributed importantly to the Camunians' sense of belonging to one and the same people. When writing came into use in the fifth or fourth century B.C., the language or dialect it expressed differed from those of neighboring lands, but it was the same from one end of the Valley to the other.

The Camonica Valley seems to have constituted a single entity socially, economically, and culturally. Except at certain extraordinary periods, its population had few contacts with the outside; it lived withdrawn unto itself, and its economy—apart from sporadic small-scale trading—was entirely confined within fixed channels. This was primarily due to the geographic situation of the country, bounded as it was by nearly impassable peaks, with only a lake and a high mountain pass as gateways to the outside world. Their ethnic and linguistic unity gave the Camunians the awareness of being a self-sufficient entity—perhaps the stirrings of a national consciousness.

9 · Conclusions

THE CAMUNIAN SOCIETY AMONG OTHER PREHISTORIC
CIVILIZATIONS OF CENTRAL EUROPE

DRIVEN BACK into its valley by the pressure of the new populations who had invaded northern Italy and the surrounding
regions during Neolithic times, the Camunian tribe managed
to continue a way of life based principally on hunting, without
being too strongly influenced by the neighboring civilizations
at the start. In the first stage Camunian art retains the schematic, abstract character of the Mesolithic, even though the
agricultural civilizations of the advanced Neolithic have already
arisen in the neighborhood. It is worth noting that the same
phenomenon occurs elsewhere in circumstances singularly like
those which pertained in the Camonica Valley.

At Mount Bego, in the Maritime Alps, Carlo Conti has
discovered the remains of human dwellings in a small cave

where carvings were found similar in style and technique to those of the first period in the Valley. He also found some ancient pottery of a type which archaeologists call cardial ware and which in Liguria and other Mediterranean areas characterizes populations of an early Neolithic cultural level. Here in the midst of the Alps it was probably made later than elsewhere and probably dates from the third millennium before Christ. This seems to suggest that at about that time a semi-barbaric group, driven from its original territory by more advanced agriculturists, took refuge in the heart of the Maritime Alps.

In the Cottian Alps, near Turin, another tribe withdrew at about the same time into a narrow and remote valley. These people, the Valdese tribe, also executed rock paintings and carvings. They constitute an exceptional ethnic phenomenon; for they have managed to remain an entity, retaining their quite distinctive personality right into our own times and preserving their traditional, religious, and historic autonomy. The Alps, as well as the French Massif Central and certain arid or peripheral regions of Europe, have thus served as refuge to aboriginal peoples when the plains were overrun by more highly developed farmers. These tribes, who had first lived in the fertile flatlands, emigrated to remote areas which would shelter them. There their lives would be more difficult, but they would be able to maintain their ancestral traditions and their way of life away from regions where contact with the more advanced and dynamic populations condemned them to assimilation and extinction.

For some reason which we cannot explain, many of the confined and isolated tribes developed a religious art and sometimes achieved exceptional mastery and beauty in it. This religious art, in its early phases, evidences an indisputable unity, suggesting a relationship, at least on a cultural plane, among the makers of menhir statues, carvings, and paintings. In the Camonica Valley and around it there are slabs that might be classed either as statues or as carvings. An instance is the three rocks at Caven, twenty miles from the Valley, which were formed and polished by the artists before being covered with carvings. Along with classic designs belonging to style III of the Valley art, they also include what are apparently characteristics of statue menhirs. In the Valley itself, at Ossimo, Professor Bonafini has uncovered a typical statue menhir with unmistakable Camunian elements.

In the neighboring region of the Upper Adige there existed at the time another tribe who wrought statue menhirs; the contacts between the Camunians of period III and this tribe, on the other side of an Alpine pass, must have been almost daily ones. The Camunian influences in the figurations of the statue menhirs from the Upper Adige bear undeniable witness to their relations. In the Valdese valley, too, paintings and carvings occur which are typologically related to one of the archaic phases of Mount Bego.

The study of the statue menhirs found in the Lunigiana near La Spezia or in Aveyron in southern France demonstrates that the ties diminish with distance, but very often a like inspiration and even similar figures or concepts are discernible in all these prehistoric works of art, seeming definitely to link them.

These works present the following patterns of diffusion when grouped according to typology and style: in northern Italy the art of the Metal Ages falls into five principal groups, three consisting of carvings and two of statues. The Bego group, centered at Mount Bego in the Maritime Alps, extends to the north as far as the Cottian Alps; carvings of a similar type have been discovered near Züschen, Hessen, and Halle, Saxony, on the polished slabs of megalithic monuments. The lower Ligurian group, studied mainly by Dr. Isetti, is related to a whole series of paintings and carvings in the south of France, analyzed by the Abbé Glory. These seem to be expressions of an art that arose originally in eastern Spain and spread from there along the Mediterranean coast into Liguria. It has characteristics in common with artistic expressions that traveled from the same birthplace into Andalusía and Estremadura. The Camonica Valley group knew no such expansion; it remained localized in the Valley itself. In style as well as character it is much closer to the rock art of southern Scandinavia than to the two Alpine groups.

The two groups of statue menhirs, that of the Upper Adige and that of the Lunigiana, are also confined to limited and well-defined regions. So are the statues of Aveyron, whose area of expansion is restricted to a particular region south of the French Massif Central. Each of these groups has individual characteristics, but the three have many common traits and a general conception which is often the same for all.

The points of resemblance between Alpine rock pictures and menhir statues are found not in the most ancient of these monuments, which date back to Neolithic and Chalcolithic times, but in the Bronze Age statues, such as some of those found in the Upper Adige.

The groups of slabs and menhir statues from Aveyron, Tarn, and Gard are linked with Camunian art principally through torque collars depicted in the same manner as those found in the monumental stones of period III. Similar collars, fashioned in a somewhat different form, are also found on the megalithic high reliefs of the Paris basin and around the necks of the guardian goddesses of the funerary caves at Marne.* These caves, however, date from before period III of Camu-

* Cf. *Bull. Soc. Prehist. Franc.*, LVII (Paris, 1960) No. 11-12, pp. 692-712.

nian art. In all these areas the torque collar is the attribute of various divinities, male, female, and of undetermined sex. In Val Camonica we are unable to establish definitely the sex of the deity connected with the torque, but the figure frequently appears as a solar deity, and it is very unlikely that here in the Bronze Age the sun was feminine. On the other hand, both the torque and the spiral "spectacle" pendant, the constant attributes of the deity, most probably were Bronze Age female ornaments. To complete the riddle, the solar deity of the monumental stones does not bear evident sexual attributes such as breasts, sex organs, or other signs found in the menhir statues. Despite the differences, however, we believe that there are several common conceptual traits between the monumental stones of style III and the menhir statues.

A separate, distinct artistic group is formed by the rock carvings and megalithic art of Atlantic Europe, from Portugal through Galicia and Asturias to Brittany and Ireland. The conceptual foundations of this art cycle are quite unlike those of Alpine art. The technique of execution is also dissimilar, and the representational approach illustrates a totally different world. Symbolism evolves here in another direction, and the gamut of subject matter illustrates other interests and concerns. However, even in this remote group we sometimes encounter solar symbols, spirals, labyrinths, and schematic human figures that seem to show some like ideological details.

Another particular group is that of southern Scandinavia. Its evolution was different from that of Val Camonica. However, at certain phases, mainly during period IV, the resemblances between the two are striking. Each attained its style through a different route, but the results are often very much alike.

These groups of rock pictures, megalithic art, and menhir statues first turned up in Neolithic times but in most cases reached their highest development during the Bronze Age. All of them seem to appear at about the same time, when central Europe was invaded by the Mediterranean agricultural peoples and the old social and economic conditions of the continent suffered a severe upheaval.

The establishment of sedentary and half-sedentary agricultural societies throughout almost all prehistoric Europe quickly weakened intergroup relations that had till then been facilitated by a nomadic and a seminomadic way of life, thus provoking an almost total disintegration of the bonds which had originally united the peoples among themselves, and eventually isolating them. The Europe of the fifth millennium had known a cultural unity which no longer existed in the second millennium. Henceforth tools, pottery, dwellings, religion, economy diverged and developed almost autonomously in each area. Except for some groups specializing in trading, who continued to live partly or completely as nomads, most societies were to be self-subsistent.

Certain major discoveries—the domestication and then the breeding of animals, metals and their uses, the wheel and its consequences: the wagon, the plow—also led to a more sedentary life, permitting man to devote himself more completely to the tilling of the earth. In future he would cling to the soil he lived on and begin to develop all the resources that the earth offered him: he would extract metal from ore, build his home with wood, and irrigate his land with water. Near the peasants' farms the workshops of blacksmiths, carpenters, and weavers would appear.

The economic and social foundations of an agricultural society were established; they would remain almost as they were then in Europe for the next forty centuries. Since that time material culture underwent only minimal changes in its broad outlines. Not until our own time has another economic revolution, begun only a few generations ago, at last transformed that structure by introducing other factors of development like the steam engine and electricity. And now we shall see the epilogue to the technological phase that has lasted four thousand years: the advent of new sources of energy and the conquest of space will finally overthrow totally the ancient economic system and definitively break the ties that still hold us to the first soil-bound civilizations.

The beginning of the Age of Metals was marked by very great cultural distinctions between neighboring tribes; the reasons for this were many. Agriculture and sedentarization led each group to a way of life based on its environment and on the resources and local means available to it. But the arrival of new populations, each constituting a different cultural constellation; their establishment in the regions they reached; and their mingling with the local populations had the effect of introducing exotic cultural elements into the indigenous civilizations. Some of the immigrant groups maintained quite intact the culture and the tradition they had brought with them, but it is indisputable that contacts occurred between them and the indigenous tribes. They were simply contacts between disparate civilizations; their effect was to stimulate ideas and aid progress. The primitive cultural unity was gone now, the unity that had seen its sunset at the beginning of the late Stone Age; but through differences and contrasts creative energy is born.

In the first half of the second millennium the Aunjetitz culture implanted itself north of the Alps. In the middle of the same millennium the local Terramara culture appeared in the Po valley. Several groups were pulled into the orbits of these cultural systems. Others, because of their geographic positions, their ethnic origins, or for reasons we do not know, managed to preserve their traditions and develop separately. This is what happened in the Camonica Valley.

The development of a civilization constitutes a highly complex process, and an infinite number of causes can be found at the roots of the changes that mark it. At a distance of three thousand years we can do no better in most cases than note the appearance or disappearance of cultural patterns; sometimes their process of transformation is manifested only by the manufacture of a new kind of ceramic or by a different method of burying the dead. We note that local characteristics sometimes marked or influenced objects traditional to the new elements of the population. We may also notice a change in anthropological elements, probably testifying to the arrival of new peoples. But the archaeological harvest is fragmentary by its very nature, too fragmentary to give grounds for positive conclusions. No one can claim, for example, to have exhumed the skeletons of all the past inhabitants of a given site. Similarly, the discovery of some foreign human type can prove very little by itself; it could mean that a visitor died and was buried there by chance. Can we be sure, however, that its presence does not attest to the establishment of a foreign group among the original dwellers, or perhaps to the arrival of a conquering people who became the rulers of the region? Data on material culture, along with linguistic data, can guide us closer to the facts; but we must recognize that the prehistoric archaeology of Europe, at least for the moment, raises more questions than it can solve.

The reader will recall that towards the end of the Bronze Age, in the last two centuries of the second millennium, the Camonica Valley had a certain number of cultural traits in common with the Urnfield civilization which at that time covered a considerable section of central Europe. This civilization mingled foreign characteristics with others local in origin. It owes its name to the fact that these people cremated their dead and sealed them in urns. We also know that they were much more expert in metalworking than all the civilizations which had lived in the same areas and that they developed more extensive sedentary settlements than any previous inhabitants of central Europe. It has often been suggested that the Urnfield people came from eastern Europe.

Does the fact that foreign influences had penetrated central Europe at the end of the second millennium necessarily imply a mass migration? We recall that these traits, when introduced into the Camonica Valley, modified the style of its art to some degree but, despite their influence, did not prevent the retention of Camunian traditions. It is quite difficult to discover the mechanism of cultural change and to decide to what extent cultural change is related to a change in population. But it does not appear that the physical character of the population of central Europe was affected then to a noticeable degree. All that can be said is that a strong eastern wind left traces in the technology. Although we know nothing about it so far, it has often been supposed that new linguistic elements, Indo-European in nature, appeared at the same time. This postulate is based on the fact that we find these elements later among peoples who in all probability are the cultural descendants of the Urnfield civilization and who, nearly a thousand years later, spoke the Indo-European tongues of the Celts.

Even accepting that possibility, if we consider the manner in which the Romans imposed their language and culture on Spain, for example, and the way a Spanish language resulted from this influence without much change in the ethnic foundations of the peoples inhabiting the country, it is clear that this phenomenon is not particularly surprising. The mechanism of change in history and prehistory may have many and various causes; military conquest of a country and mass migration are certainly not the only possibilities. We can readily imagine others simply by watching what is happening around us today—for example, transformations of an economic and even of an ideological order. In populations which were numerically smaller and geographically more concentrated than modern nations, the possibilities must have been even greater because the degree of cultural mobility was much higher.

But, of course, we do not know exactly what happened in those distant times. We see the results; we register cultural changes. What more can we say positively?

In the first half of the first millennium relations between the Camunians and their neighbors grew more frequent and more productive. It was under the influence of such Urnfield-derived civilizations as Hallstatt and Golasecca that the Camunians learned to work iron. During this period they probably had daily contacts with tribes from north of the Alps; comparable modes of life and religious concepts resulted.

The ever-growing demand for metal ore, particularly for iron ore, impelled the Alpine populations to increase their contacts, to develop and regulate their trade. An enrichment resulted which gradually transformed the whole social structure; tribal chieftains, miners, and blacksmiths eventually came to form new privileged social classes. Soon the lack of political stability, the struggles among different tribes, and the expansion of certain civilizations (of which the Etruscan was the most important) favored the appearance of a military caste because of the constant menace against roads and frontiers. Strength would henceforth determine the relations of the peoples of the region, and each would be obliged to defend its territory, its villages, and especially its mines, source of the precious metal. These local struggles between petty kings or tribal chieftains are reminiscent of the rivalries of medieval princes determined to enlarge their own domains at the expense of their neighbors. In fact, society at that period, with its warriors, its merchants, and its craftsmen, presents many points of similarity with the Middle Ages.

Rome imposed its peace, and its reign put an end to the ephemeral ambitions of the small Alpine tribes, to their provincial nationalism, newly born and developing with incredible swiftness. This instability and the civil wars among the different ethnic groups of the region certainly facilitated conquest by the Roman legions. Such are the broad outlines of the still scarcely known history of the peoples who inhabited the valleys of the Alps during the two thousand years before our era, of whom the Camunians were part.

THE EVOLUTION OF DAILY LIFE

In two thousand years the way of life and the cultural level of Camunian society underwent appreciable transformations. New artistic and religious concepts appeared and developed; the economy changed its nature and came to be founded on different bases; the social organization was completely remodeled several times. The earlier Camunian society, consisting of small patriarchal clans, evolved into more complex political units. In the realm of religion a specialized clergy arose. They were to take an active role in Camunian life; as educators and judges, their function was to maintain equilibrium within the group.

Craftsmanship and trade, bringing wealth and special

status, created a new conception of authority and changed the notion of chief. The warriors, on whom the security or strength of the tribe depended, succeeded in acquiring greater and greater importance, until they formed a privileged group. What was left, then, of the primitive social organization of the Camonica Valley at the dawn of its history? From its original barbaric cultural level, the little community almost succeeded in reaching a stage of urban civilization. When the Roman legions arrived in the Valley, they found there fully developed villages like Cividate Camuno.

The evolution had been rapid, often even abrupt. It was sometimes heralded by external signs; vestiges of the old social order, like flotsam, were still visible in later periods beneath the new surface. But it was as though Camunian society had developed in a crescendo rhythm which started slowly and then accelerated. External influences, discoveries, peculiar economic situations, exceptional personalities perhaps—were the germs of more rapid transformation and even of some abrupt mutations in Camunian history. Through the detection, collection, and analysis of the available facts we are able to piece together an astonishing picture of a little Alpine tribe during more than two thousand years of existence.

The historical and social changes observed in the Camonica Valley have a great many parallels elsewhere. They illustrate rather accurately the march of Europe in Neolithic times and in the Metal Ages. There were no two identical population groups; but, apart from a few exceptions, all these groups progressed in like fashion and by the same routes: from a simple to a complex economy, from a patriarchal society organized in clans to an urban society of specialists.

In the economic realm the Camunian civilization was an exception, however, for it always remained mainly a society of hunters and craftsmen. Agriculture and stockfarming had only secondary importance there until the Roman period, whereas for many societies in the same area these two activities were essential. The Camunian economy underwent fluctuations; we have seen how external commerce and external relations varied with the times. Moreover, a succession of political influences were felt in the Valley: the Remedello civilization; the Mycenaeans; the Urnfield peoples; the Etruscans; and finally the Romans.

Innumerable gaps remain in the history of the Camunians. But their art reveals what is found nowhere else in Europe—the complete chronological outline of a people's development during more than two thousand years, from the Stone Age to Roman times, from savagery to civilization.

WHAT THE ROCKS SAY

When I came to the Camonica Valley for the first time six years ago, I was indeed a long way from imagining the extraordinary testimony hidden in the woods and meadows under moss and soil. If I had some intimation of the value of the discovery, I had not the least idea of its richness nor of its antiquity. How could I—the first rocks my collaborators and I studied represented nothing more than animal and human figures in various poses. Only the weapons and implements pictured gave a vague indication of the age of the carvings. Not until we had gathered an immense array of iconographic data, had undertaken its analysis and then attempted an initial synthesis, did the darkness of centuries finally begin to dissipate, the history of the Valley and its civilization to emerge in rough outline, and finally the clear vision of what we had uncovered, to appear.

But the study of the Camunian rocks is still only beginning. The carvings we have uncovered are not all that exist. There are others, still entombed, which must be found and studied, too.

The future will probably oblige us to change, abandon, or correct some of the hypotheses we have proposed here. But for now we can be confident that we know at least the general characteristics of Camunian civilization: its development, the way of life of the Valley's dwellers, their economic and social systems, their religion, and their thought.

Standing before the storied rocks to which the Camunians entrusted their heritage, we feel as though the worshippers, laborers, sorcerers, priests, chieftains, and warriors of this ancient people are speaking to us and telling us their tale. The role of the historian, of the archaeologist, of the ethnologist consists simply in trying to understand them with a dedicated patience and a sincere interest. A bond is then created between them and us: before our eyes unfold two thousand years of life in that Alpine valley; and in the everyday problems of this people, in their beliefs, in their social relations we discern our own image. These men were very like us; by trying to understand them it is ourselves we discover. In studying the development of their world it is the mystery of our own that we may illuminate.

The reader will have noticed that certain events in Camunian history are of contemporary significance and can be compared to what is happening before our very eyes or what happened a few generations ago: the replacement of druids and sorcerers by warriors; the birth of a primitive capitalism at a time of highest commercial development; the growing power of the chief over the community; the wars among the region's tribes for control over an iron mine or an important transit route; and finally the disappearance of all the tiny

political entities which were those tribes, and their engulfment by the Roman Empire. In these events we have little
difficulty in recognizing our own century. A humanity constantly in evolution, a perpetual struggle for progress and for
the conquest of new intellectual and geographic realms—these
problems and situations reappear at all times. "One generation passeth away, and another generation cometh: but the
earth abideth forever. . . . The thing that hath been, it is
that which shall be; and that which is done is that which
shall be done: and there is no new thing under the sun."
Thus spake Ecclesiastes, King of Jersusalem. . . .

Index

References to illlustrations are given in parentheses

i

EMMANUEL ANATI was born in Florence, Italy, in 1930. He migrated to Israel in 1945, fought in the Israeli Army in 1948-9, and then began to study archaeology at the Hebrew University in Jerusalem, where he obtained his B.A. in 1953 and his M.A. in 1955. He directed several projects for the Israel Department of Antiquities, including the excavations of the Bronze Age cemetery of Tell Abu Hawam and a survey of the Negev Desert, where he came across an area containing hitherto unknown prehistoric rock carvings in 1954. This aroused his interest in prehistoric art. His articles on the discovery of these pictures in that region brought him a fellowship from the French Government, and studies in ethnology at the Sorbonne in 1956-8, leading eventually to the degree of *Docteur ès lettres* in 1960. During the period of his studies in France, Mr. Anati led expeditions in southern France, Spain, and Italy, for research on prehistoric art, for the Centre National de la Recherche Scientifique, Paris. He then visited the United States and, in 1959, obtained his M.A. in anthropology and social relations from Harvard, contributing work on prehistoric art in the Alps and Liguria to the American Philosophical Society, 1959-60.

In 1960 he undertook a further research project in the Negev Desert, with a grant from the Wenner-Gren Foundation for Anthropological Research. Mr. Anati has published a book in Hebrew on *The Archaeological Periods in Israel* (1957) and about forty papers on prehistoric and primitive art in scientific journals in the United States, England, France, Italy, and Israel. His home is in Jerusalem.

August 1961

A NOTE ON THE TYPE

THIS BOOK is set in ELECTRA, a Linotype face designed by the late W. A. Dwiggins (1880-1956). This face cannot be classified as either modern or old-style. It is not based on any historical model, nor does it echo any particular period or style. It avoids the extreme contrasts between thick and thin elements that mark most modern faces, and attempts to give a feeling of fluidity, power, and speed.

Composed by Publishers' Composition Service,
Brattleboro, Vermont.
Printed by The Murray Printing Company,
Forge Village, Mass.
Paper made by Mead Papers Inc., New York.
Bound by H. Wolff, New York.
Typography and binding design by
VINCENT TORRE